CW00384347

I Think I P
Tinned Variety

The Diary of a Petty Officer in the Fleet Air Arm during World War II

N Buckle and C Murray

In memory of Norman Buckle (1924 - 1978)

Copyright © C Murray 2012
All Rights Reserved

"The oranges' season is now well in and the crop is excellent. Pineapples are also in and I had my first the other day. They are quite juicy but rather woody. I think I prefer the tinned variety."

From the diary of N Buckle FX585169 20th January 1944

CONTENTS

I Think I Prefer the Tinned Variety

The Diary of a Petty Officer

in the Fleet Air Arm during World War II

Introduction

My father, Norman Buckle, was nineteen years old when in 1943 he arrived in West Africa as a wartime volunteer in the Fleet Air Arm of the Royal Navy. He came from a coal mining village in South Yorkshire and he'd never been abroad before. He was one of the thousands of young men (even boys) who had not only never left Britain but had rarely visited anywhere in their own country either. Apart from day trips to nearby towns and cycle rides to country places, Norman had only been on holiday to seaside resorts such as Morecambe, Blackpool (where his Auntie Beatty kept a boarding house), Scarborough and Cowes in the Isle of Wight. Like the vast majority of those war-time recruits he had no sea-going experience and found naval shore bases and the ships of the fleet to be alien environments with their own customs, vocabulary and technologies. Although it was expressly forbidden by the naval authorities, Norman kept a personal diary during his service which documents some of his experiences, thoughts and emotions. He died in 1978 aged fifty four years and his war time diary remained stored in an old suitcase in several lofts and attics for over thirty years.

After I retired I spent many a happy hour researching both my own and my husband's family histories. Eventually though, I came to a dead end after I had explored every aspect of the lives of even the most distant relatives. I had already sorted through a box of old photos that had been in the loft for years and had labelled as many of them as I could. Now I turned my attention to an old, homemade, hard backed notebook with the initials N.B. stencilled on the deteriorating hessian cover. I knew that this was a collection of photographs and postcards that my dad had stuck in the book accompanied by captions in his tiny, precise handwriting. Folded into the book were lots of pages torn from an old diary for 1944 and several sheets of notepaper covered in that same spidery handwriting.

I'd read all of this many years previously and knew that it recorded his time at a Royal Navy airbase known as His Majesty's Ship (H.M.S.) Spurwing in Hastings, near Freetown, Sierra Leone, West Africa. It also covered the weeks he'd spent in Australia prior to being sent to Ponam in the Admiralty Islands (part of present day Papua New Guinea). I read it again and was intrigued by what my dad had written and as I deciphered his handwriting a number of questions were raised in my mind. I decided to type up the manuscript to make the extracts more legible and accessible and then passed copies to my two sisters. Like me, they were intrigued and also prompted to ask questions in relation to what they were reading. When he was alive, our dad had never really spoken about his war time experiences and when we were younger we hadn't been interested in what he'd been doing thirty years previously. Now we had the interest we didn't have the person with the answers.

I decided to use the skills I'd acquired in pursuing our family histories to track down more of the background to our dad's war. The more I read and the more of the background I understood, the more interested I became. I paid for a copy of dad's records from the Royal Navy Archives but these gave incomplete details of his service. Then my sister discovered in her loft, in another old suitcase, a folder containing the original documents that were his Fleet Air Arm records: they detailed in chronological order where he'd been and what his role was. There were other documents that added further to his story.

Norman's diary is a record of the mundane and the extraordinary. It gives insights into the colonial attitudes of ordinary people. Before World War II, Britain was a maritime super-power with an empire of thirteen million square miles and a population of five hundred and thirty million people. Yet as the war went on, Britain's survival depended increasingly on support from the United States of America and British imperial superiority was fading fast. Nevertheless the service personnel sent out to Africa and other colonial areas continued to act out the role of imperial masters; they travelled to many countries and experienced a variety of climates, conditions, customs and cultures that the majority had hardly imagined and certainly never expected to experience. The language used in some parts of Norman's diary is not what we would use to-day. It epitomises the colonial attitudes of the era and I have left it in the diary un-edited because it is of its time and a true reflection of how things were then, even though in places it is quite shocking. Norman was interested in the people, the history and the geography of the places he visited. He was curious and inquiring and this can be seen in some of the entries in his diary. But he was nevertheless only a young man and he sometimes found the behaviours and actions of his fellow naval colleagues as alien and challenging as those of the indigenous peoples of the places he visited.

I hope that my annotations enhance the diary and make it even more interesting without interfering with the snapshot of an era that the diary embodies. A collection of original photos of H.M.S. Spurwing, Hastings, near Freetown, Sierra Leone (1943 - 44) and H.M.S. Nabaron, (MONAB 4), Ponam Island, The Admiralty Islands, British Pacific Fleet (1945) can be viewed at Spurwing ebooks http://www.spurwing-ebooks.com.

Norman was a working class lad who was born in 1924 and brought up in the village of Royston, near Barnsley, in South Yorkshire. He was fortunate, having passed his eleven plus, to have enough family support to go to the local grammar school at Normanton. He was studious, worked hard and passed his School Certificate. At the age of sixteen he was offered employment as a clerk at the salary of £1 - 0s - 0d per week (about £30 in to-day's money) in the Public Health Department of the West Riding County Council in Wakefield thus breaking three generations of the family's tradition of going down the pit. His father, grandfather and great grandfather all worked at the local colliery and his paternal grandfather had been an under-manager at the pit. However it was Norman's mother who was the source of aspiration; she had a sister who was an assistant school teacher at Royston Infant School and her father was the inspector for the Royston section of the Barnsley Canal. They lived at Bridge House in Royston which is still there today although the canal is disused and overgrown.

15th October 1942 Joined the Fleet Air Arm of the Royal Navy

War had already been declared when Norman started his new job in October 1940. In August 1942 he volunteered to join the Royal Navy opting for the Fleet Air Arm. Folded up in his diary is a page torn out of the weekly edition of "The Times," dated 11th December 1940, entitled "On Board An Aircraft Carrier" which includes photographs of a "Walrus" type aircraft being prepared for action. The text explains that the activities of the Fleet Air Arm in the Mediterranean were outstanding. I wonder if it was this article that inspired Norman to try for the Fleet Air Arm.

The Royal Navy had an air section from 1903 which was utilised during the First World War for spotting, signalling and reconnaissance. It was combined in 1918 with the Royal Flying Corps to form the Royal Air Force. By 1919, naval air power had been hugely reduced to a very small number of aircraft: reconnaissance planes, torpedo bombers, fighter planes, sea planes and flying boats. In 1924 there was a policy change at the Admiralty and it was decided that all observers and 70% of pilots of navy planes would be naval personnel. In February 1927 the name of Naval Air Branch was instituted and by July 1937 all aircraft in warships were back under the control of the Admiralty. By May 1939 the Admiralty had full and complete control of all naval flying and with its Headquarters at Lee-on-Solent, in Hampshire, the Fleet Air Arm was born.

During the early months of World War II, the policy makers at the Admiralty thought that naval battleships were what would be needed to win the war and they were slow to grasp the necessity for a rapid expansion of the Fleet Air Arm. Little attempt had been made to equip the Royal Navy with fighter planes or radar and a desperate deal was done with the United States Navy for a supply of planes. Equally there was a chronic shortage of aircraft carriers and a conversion programme for merchant ships and grain carriers was put in place.

At its inception the Fleet Air Arm was comprised of just 20 squadrons with only 232 aircraft. As the war years progressed, Fleet Air Arm aircraft numbers increased culminating in the greatest concentration of British naval air power ever seen. The crippling of the Italian Fleet in Taranto Harbour in 1940 was the Fleet Air Arm's greatest success in the early phase of World War II. The Fleet Air Arm was also responsible for counter attacks on the U Boats which threatened British convoys in the Atlantic. However, its outstanding contribution was in the war against Japan alongside the United States, Australian and New Zealand navies. By the end of the war, the Fleet Air Arm had 59 aircraft carriers, 3,700 aircraft, 72,000 officers and men and 56 naval air stations.

Norman was signed up as a war-time volunteer on 15th October 1942 and his official registration papers show that he had volunteered "until the end of the period of the present emergency". He is described as 6 ft and 3/8 inch tall, 34 inch chest, light brown hair, blue eyes, mid-pale complexion with a mole in the right dorsal and lumber regions. He was allocated to the Fleet Air Arm. He was 18 years and 6 months old when along with so many other young men he went to H.M.S. Royal Arthur for induction training into the Royal Navy. Norman was then transferred for seven months to shore bases H.M.S. Shrapnel and H.M.S. Ariel to train as a Radio Mechanic. Once qualified he spent three months at another shore base, H.M.S. Condor, before being sent on 9th October 1943 to H.M.S. Waxwing to await his first posting overseas.

It was while waiting for his first posting abroad that Norman began to write his diary.

Saturday 9th October 1943

"Arrived back at Waxwing from leave about 10.30 after travelling up with Harold Simpson who was going up to Crail on a pilot's course.

Discovered I was due to leave on following Wednesday.

Duty watch so unable to go ashore at night."

H.M.S Waxwing was a Royal Navy transit camp at Townhill, near Dunfermline, Scotland. Crail was a Royal Naval Air Station (R.N.A.S.) in Fife, Scotland known as H.M.S. Jackdaw. It was in use from October 1940 until April 1947 and was used for air torpedo training.

Sunday 10th October 1943

"Strange to have divisions again on Sunday morning as I have not been used to it for over three months at Arbroath.

Went to Edinburgh this afternoon and for a change went via ferry. By this means one gets a wonderful view of the Forth Bridge and realises its immense size.

Went for tea on arrival in Edinburgh and after met Eddie and went to Garrison Theatre. Not particularly good.

Fish and chips after and then a walk on Castle Hill until time for train. The hill was crowded with large numbers of Yanks, Canadians, Poles etc., in various stages of sexual excitement. A disgusting spectacle.

Rained all the way from Dunfermline to Townhill."

For "Divisions" all personnel were expected whether on board ship or at a shore base to assemble together standing with the division to which they were attached. It was the responsibility of each divisional Petty Officer to ensure that everyone who was supposed to be there actually was present and to check up later on any absentees. The Petty Officers then reported to the Divisional Lieutenant who would undertake a full inspection of all the men, looking out for anyone who appeared dishevelled or unwell or for signs of indiscipline. Divisional officers would then report all present to the Commander who in turn would report to the Captain and then the process of "divisions" was complete. It was a survival from the days of sail when it was necessary in the morning to check up that no one had fallen overboard in the night.

"Arbroath" refers to H.M.S. Condor - a naval air station situated at Arbroath near Dundee, Scotland. From July to September 1943 Norman's duties here as a Leading Radio Mechanic were in Squadron Maintenance. "Leading" in this context is the naval equivalent of a corporal in the army; a Petty Officer is the naval equivalent of a sergeant in the army. While Norman was working at Arbroath, the aircraft from the British carrier H.M.S. Victorious were all flown in for repair and maintenance after their successful contribution to the Pacific war effort with the United States Navy. The Americans had gone to war with Japan after Pearl Harbour in December 1941 and the British contribution to the Pacific war was small at that stage because of the huge strain on the Royal Navy in other theatres of war. Victorious was taken out of service for a re-fit and my speculation is that's why Norman was sent to Arbroath. A team of maintenance personnel kept the planes air-worthy. The Radio Mechanic's job was to remove the aircraft's heavy radio set for testing and repair and then after re-placing the radio set in the aircraft go on a test flight to check the radio was working properly. Some of the mechanics were trained as wireless operators who had to use Morse code but that wasn't part of Norman's job. H.M.S. Condor was nicknamed "Aberbrothock" and had been commissioned in June 1940. It had space for 200 aircraft and in addition to aircraft maintenance it was a training establishment for naval aviation specialising in training Observers (the naval term for navigators) and it also had a deck landing school. Later it had an air signals school as well.

Royal Navy shore bases (both barracks and training establishments) were sometimes known as "stone frigates". They were usually situated near to the coast so that the planes could fly ashore before the aircraft carrier got into harbour and still remain operational. All shore bases were known by the title of Royal Naval Air Station (R.N.A.S.) and the name of the town or village where they were located. They were also all given an H.M.S. name. For example H.M.S. Condor was also known as R.N.A.S. Arbroath; H.M.S. Spurwing was R.N.A.S. Hastings (Freetown). The Admiralty used bird names for shore bases keeping the traditional and heroic names for the ships of the fleet. However, the shore bases were organised as though they were a ship at sea. Throughout this book I intend to use the H.M.S. name for all shore bases but make it clear where they were located.

Monday 11th October 1943

"Gunnery lectures all day and duty watch at night.

Rather stupid that during one's last days in England (or rather Scotland) for, maybe years, one is not allowed out of barbed wire for one day in two."

Tuesday 12th October 1943

"Gunnery morning and afternoon.

Out on the first liberty boat and sausage, chips and cake for tea.

"Star Spangled Rhythm" after and then supper at Y.M.C.A. Unfortunately, their radiogram has broken down so cannot play any records.

Looking forward to tomorrow, although not without some qualms as to what the future holds in store."

"Star Spangled Rhythm" was a 1943 all-star musical film made by Paramount Pictures during World War II as a morale booster. Stars in the cast included Bob Hope, Bing Crosby, Fred MacMurray, Dorothy Lamour, Paulette Goddard, Veronica Lake and Dick Powell.

During World War II the volunteers of the "Y.M.C.A." (Young Men's Christian Association) were involved in running hostels, rest-rooms and canteen services for the troops. They provided books, athletic equipment and musical instruments for the overseas troops rest-rooms. They operated mobile canteen vans staffed and driven mainly by Y.M.C.A. women volunteers. They also attended to the spiritual needs of the troops.

Wednesday 13th October 1943

"Drafting routine all morning.

Medical and dental inspections but no inoculations, thank goodness.

Shook hands all round and left Waxwing about 3.30 in the afternoon. The radio mechanics with me are Chuck, John and Bill for Freetown, Joe and Bob for Gibraltar and Pete for the Indomitable. [H.M.S. Indomitable - an aircraft carrier built at Barrow-in-Furness in 1937 by Vickers-Armstrong.]

Left Dunfermline on the 4.45p.m. for Glasgow. As we went over the Forth Bridge threw a halfpenny over for luck, although I reckon that won't be much good if we get "tinfished" in the Bay. ["Tinfished" means being sunk by a torpedo.]

Supper in Glasgow to the music of Beethoven's Mass and then a walk round the town until 11.15. Damned the immortal souls of the heathenish Scots when we discovered the pubs closed at 9 o'clock but managed to consume quite an amount in the two hours at our disposal.

Wrote a letter home on the train and posted it at Liverpool. Had breakfast at Liverpool Y.M.C.A. about 07.00 then waited until 10.30 for a lorry to the docks.

Saw the London train go out and Pete almost burst into tears. He's only just got married on his draft leave and it must be hard on him."

Thursday 14th October 1943

"Transport arrived, picked us up and dumped us on the wharf alongside "S.S. Orbita" an armed merchant cruiser used as a troop carrier.

Climbed the stairs (damned if I know the nautical name) and then, after finding ourselves on the top deck, tried to find our mess, which we were told was "just forrard".

Eventually discovered it and found it to be a place about the size of a single tennis court where 360 of us were to eat and sleep for Heavens knows how long - not a very pleasant prospect.

Lousy dinner, tea and supper and then prepared to lash a hammock for the first time in my life. Made a horrible mess of it and then, after bruising myself from head to foot, managed finally to get into it.

Spent a most uncomfortable night with my neck and feet getting mixed up in the clews [the cords by which a hammock is suspended] and with crowds of stokers and seamen snoring, spitting and doing various other things all around.

If this is going to sea give me a nice quiet land station anytime. At the last moment, Pete was sent back to Glasgow to pick up the Indom. at Greenock."

S.S. (Steam Ship) Orbita was an ocean liner built in 1914 by Harland and Wolff in Belfast to provide transatlantic passenger transport. In the early nineteen twenties she was used for the Royal Mail's London to New York service before reverting to passenger transport in 1926. From 1941 until the end of World War II she was used for transporting troops. After the war she was used for transporting immigrants to Australia and New Zealand. She also transported, after the Empire Windrush in 1948, the second group of emigrants from the West Indies to the U.K. S.S. Orbita was finally dismantled in 1950.

Friday 15th October 1943 Off to Sea

"Cast off about noon and then anchored for the rest of the day out in the estuary.

Exactly one year today since I joined the Navy....."

Exactly one year before this diary entry on 15th October 1942 Norman had arrived at H.M.S. Royal Arthur, a shore establishment of the Royal Navy at Skegness. Previously a Butlin's holiday camp it was commissioned as a training establishment in 1939 for new naval recruits.

The holiday camp had opened in April 1936 and was the first of the camps designed by Billy Butlin to provide affordable, luxurious holidays for working people. For 35 shillings a week holiday makers could enjoy three meals a day and free entertainment. On the outbreak of war, the camp was immediately taken over by the Royal Navy and painted in dull naval colours. The Sick Bay was accommodated in the indoor Beer Garden; the dentist got the Fortune Teller's parlour; the Viennese Dance Hall was turned into the armoury packed with rifles; and the recruits were accommodated in the holiday chalets.

During their training the recruits were allocated to a trade and taught the discipline, routines and language of naval life. They were expected to be self-sufficient and to learn to get on with each other regardless of where they'd come from or what their background was. German Radio claimed on more than one occasion that H.M.S. Royal Arthur had been sunk!

On completion of basic training Norman was classified as an Ordinary Telegrapher and sent for further training from 13 November 1942 to 20 March 1943 at H.M.S. Shrapnel (Walthamstow). This was actually the South West Essex Technical College and School of Art opened in 1938. It was used during World War II by the armed services to provide technical training for personnel. The Royal Navy took it over in 1942 when it was re-classified as a ship and called H.M.S. Shrapnel. Norman was to become a radio mechanic for which the training included: General Electrical Practice, General Wireless Telegraphy Practice, Special Pulse Circuits and Workshops. After this period of instruction he was examined and awarded a pass with 53% even though the pass rate was 65%!

Norman made the most of the opportunity of being based near to London. After the onslaught of the Blitz, there had been a lull in the bombing. Then, in November 1942, as part of the so-called Baedeker Raids, the bombing of London started again with a further 1,600 fatalities. In addition to London, Hitler had ordered the Luftwaffe to attack some of Britain's historic cities such as Canterbury, Exeter, Norwich and Bath ostensibly selected from a Baedeker Guide to the British Isles. Even so, this didn't put Norman off and he visited London as often as he could enjoying the bookshops and concert halls of the West End.

From 21 March 1943 to 20 June 1943 Norman was sent to H.M.S. Ariel, the Royal Navy Air Radio and Air Mechanics Training Establishment at Warrington. Here the training for Radio Mechanics included Theory, Fault Finding, Making Good Defects and Setting Up. This time he passed with 71% overall and, as the required pass rate was 60%, on completion of his training he was promoted to the position of Leading Radio Mechanic.

He had been stationed at H.M.S. Waxwing for a couple of weeks before being sent on his first naval employment to H.M.S. Condor.

So exactly one year later, Norman's diary continues.

Friday 15th October 1943 (cont.)

"…..An interesting year - all the new work on radio and radio location, square bashing at Skegness, concerts at the Albert Hall, book-hunting in Charing Cross Road, duets with Alfie at "Ariel", organ at Arbroath, first sight of Forth and Tay bridges, Carnegie Park at Dunfermline - one of the most interesting of my life so far.

Another sleepless night."

Saturday 16th October 1943

"Weighed anchor and away by 10.00.

Sailing all day.

Routine on board extremely easy - clean up until about 09.00 and then the rest of the day free.

Passed the coast of Northern Ireland."

Sunday 17th October 1943

"Picked up a convoy somewhere off Ireland - 12 vessels.

As we get further into the Atlantic the ship rolls and heaves more and more.

Fried eggs at breakfast produces a queer feeling in stomach."

The sinking of the S.S. Athenia by a German U-boat in the North Atlantic in September 1939 occasioned huge amounts of public anger. Consequently, merchant ships were organised into convoys, and routes were established to try and ensure the safe arrival of supplies, weaponry and troops. Merchant shipping had to make sure that food and the essential supplies for British industry and the war effort from all over the world were maintained. The efforts to keep the Atlantic crossings open and safe were crucial to success and the belief was widely held that if the war at sea was lost so was the whole war. A system of convoys had been introduced towards the end of World War I where groups of merchant ships would travel together across the Atlantic. The convoy system was already in place again by the end of 1939 and as the war progressed it was developed and became increasingly complex. Convoys were organised across the Atlantic from North America to Britain and also down the coast of West Africa to Freetown, Sierra Leone and on to South Africa, India and Singapore and the reverse. During 1940 there was minimal protection for convoys and an early sonar detection system for submarines was found to be ineffective. Desperate for escort vessels a deal had been made in 1940 with the neutral U.S. Government to exchange the rights to use British bases in the Caribbean for fifty old warships surplus to American requirements. As the war progressed and American attitudes changed, President Roosevelt enacted, on 11th March 1941, the Bill to Further Promote the Defence of the United States which brought into being the Lend-Lease scheme and effectively ended American neutrality. Through the scheme the U.S.A. lent vast amounts of munitions, ships, vehicles, and food supplies to Britain, China and later the Soviet Union. The terms of the scheme were that the equipment supplied was to be used until it was time for its return. Roosevelt wanted the American people to get on board with the idea and he used the analogy of what you would do if your neighbour's house was burning down and you owned a garden hose. He asked, would you try to sell it to your neighbour for the price you'd paid for it or would you lend it to them as quickly as possible and have it returned after the emergency had passed? To which Senator Taft of Ohio responded by pointing out that lending war equipment was similar to lending chewing gum in that you wouldn't want it back!

Wednesday 20th October 1943

"Had my first meal since Sunday and managed by dint of perseverance to keep it down. We are now somewhere in the middle of the North Atlantic and the cold is intense.

This together with the remains of sea sickness makes life intolerable."

Saturday 23rd October 1943

"Ordinary routine for the last two days.

Early this morning, sighted the rocky, mountainous coast of Africa, and steamed up it until we came in sight of Gibraltar.

In the distance the rock looked exactly like the picture on a postage stamp, but as we approached closer it became bigger until by the time we were underneath, it towered above us.

No shore leave.

The side facing us is extremely steep. The top is covered with green bushes and among them one can make out mounds of earth which must be gun emplacements.

The town itself is on the lower slopes and consists of tiers of streets of houses, all built in yellow stone in the Moroccan style - semicircular arches, balconies, verandas and pinnacles etc.

The sea is an intense blue colour and the mountains across the straits look very near at hand, although they are about 13 miles away.

The strategic importance of the rock is obvious. Its guns commanding the whole of the entrance to the Med.

One of our chaps who went ashore on ship's business told us that fruit was very scarce. Bananas and oranges at 6d each.

At night the harbour was illuminated. There is no blackout at all and the whole town is lit up.

I feel rather sorry for Bob and Joe having to stay here for 3 years as I should think it will be very monotonous."

Sunday 24th October 1943

"A beautiful morning with church on board.

Watched divisions on a nearby cruiser and very pretty it looked. Everyone in white, White Ensign blowing in the breeze and the chaplain in his long surplice.

Extremely hot in the afternoon. A taste of things to come.

Left Gib. at about 16.00 and steamed down the coast of what I suppose is Spanish Morocco.

Could not sleep for sunburn at night."

The White Ensign is the British flag used at sea and in shore establishments by the Royal Navy. It consists of a red St George's cross on a white background with a Union Flag in the upper left quarter.

Monday 25th October 1943

"Arrived at Casablanca about 10.00.

Stayed two hours while our escort destroyers re-fuelled.

Continued to sea.

Changed to tropical rig in afternoon - khaki shirt and shorts. Many comments at this from R.N. chaps as the Fleet Air Arm is the only branch of Navy allowed khaki in the tropics.

The nights are extremely beautiful. I stood in the bows for a long time tonight watching the sunset and the swarms of flying fish playing in the spray. Some of them are quite large and their mode of travel is to swim until they are moving very fast and then launch themselves with a flick of the tail and glide just above the water. A school of porpoises followed for quite a while."

Sunday 31st October 1943 Freetown, Sierra Leone, West Africa

"Sighted the African coast early in the morning and at 10.10 dropped anchor in Freetown harbour.

The town looks very pretty with brightly coloured houses, the outstanding objects being a church and two wireless aerials. Behind the town to the left is the coastal range of hills.

Large numbers of canoes fill the harbour, some mere dug-outs but others quite decent boats.

All the natives are asking for pennies and when refused swear in a most horrible manner. At 16.30 the launch arrives to take us ashore and our kit is unloaded by small boys.

We no sooner set foot ashore than scores of boys and girls mob us selling bananas. The first one tastes good.

After a long wait a lorry appears to take us to a place called Hastings where the Air Station is, its commissioned name being H.M.S. Spurwing.

We drive at a breathless pace through the streets containing hordes of gaudily dressed natives, open air stalls selling peanuts, brightly lit churches and chapels. There is no blackout at all.

Soon we leave the town behind and the headlights show a narrow road lined with palm trees with occasional thatched huts with open fires outside.

The road winds up and down over narrow bridges and round hair pin bends until we arrive at a small village which we are told is called Kissy.

We do not stay but rush on until after an hour's travel we turn down a side track, past a cemetery and pull up against a bungalow which is the Regulatory Office of H.M.S. Spurwing.

We have arrived at the end of our journey."

Freetown is the capital and largest city of Sierra Leone, West Africa. It has the third largest natural harbour in the world. During World War II, Freetown was crucial in the convoy route from Britain to South Africa, India and Australia. The base served a total of thirty two different convoy routes. It was home to large warships of the Royal Navy, destroyer escorts and submarines. The ocean off the West Coast of Africa was a hunting ground for German submarines.

The high temperatures and humidity made a posting to Freetown very unpopular with services personnel and it had become known as "the white man's grave" because it was surrounded by malarial mangrove swamps. The humidity was so high that if a pair of shoes was left unattended underneath a bed, in a week it would be covered with green mould.

Hastings is fifteen miles east of Freetown and an aerodrome had been constructed there from which Fleet Air Arm planes operated. 710 Squadron was formed in August 1939 as a seaplane squadron searching for U boats attacking convoys and commercial shipping. Later, 777 Squadron was formed at Hastings on 1st August 1941 as a fleet requirements unit. It had a small number of Swordfish aircraft to which Defiants and Walruses were added in 1942. Throughout 1943 the squadron was responsible for the air defence of Sierra Leone. A civil aerodrome nearby at Freetown was operated by the R.A.F.

H.M.S. Spurwing was a shore base hacked out of the bush at Hastings, near Freetown. It was commissioned in March 1943 and had capacity for eighty four aircraft. According to his service record, Norman's job at H.M.S. Spurwing was A.S.U. (Aircraft Storage Unit) Maintenance.

After the 16 day voyage from Scotland to Sierra Leone, Norman didn't write any more in his diary for several weeks. It's amazing to think how long it took to get there when flying time nowadays is about six and a half hours.

Saturday 1st January 1944

"New Year's Day. Rang in the New Year well and truly on the ship's bell. Nearly all the officers and ratings were in various stages of inebriation.

The first lieutenant vainly trying to drink someone's health from a bottle with the top still on.

Foul taste in mouth in morning due to excess of port wine.

Cinema at night."

Sunday 2nd January 1944

"Served at Mass for the first time in many months. Four communicants.

Whist drive at night and much to my surprise won a prize for the highest number of fives."

Monday 3rd January 1944

"Rising at 06.00 comes as a shock after two days of lying in but we recover.

Messing about all morning with P.D. gear."

It is unclear what Norman meant by P.D. gear. One possible explanation is photographic development equipment: he certainly had his own camera with him and may have been able to access what he needed to develop his photos. Another explanation is positive displacement gear. The principle of positive displacement had been established in the nineteenth century and by the mid-twentieth century had a number of applications including the positive displacement blower. A version of this was the vapour compressor which was needed in World War II to ensure that a dependable supply of fresh water was always readily available on ships and shore bases with very basic facilities. The most popular way to create fresh water was to heat stale water: the vacuum created by the vapour compressor extracted the steam which was then condensed into fresh water. This process was called the Kleinschmidt cycle. Possibly the equipment was temperamental and Norman and anyone else who had time to spare and some appropriate knowledge would tinker with it.

"Freetown in afternoon. With Chuck. Spent a pleasant time in a Syrian shop looking at cloths, silks, scents – a woman's paradise. Prices exorbitant but only to be expected in such circumstances e.g. Dressing gown £3.3, printed cloth 4/- a yard, torches 7/6.

As usual accosted by a young native with promises of "jig-jig". Amused himself by calling us white bastards when refused. The coast natives are a very ignorant crowd being mostly the descendents of released slaves and having no tribal laws and customs which usually are good and sensible. Prostitution is rife and there are any number of brothels, some of which, I am sorry to say, are patronised by our men, which seems to me very degrading for both white and black.

Recovered by the sight of eggs and chips for tea.

Short account of the Crown Colony of Sierra Leone

As my stay, up to the present has been confined to the coastal regions, all my observations will be on this area.

Physical Appearance

The first object that catches the eye on nearing the colony is the range of mountains from which the colony takes its name (Lion Mountain). The reference to Lion is obscure as there is no visible resemblance, but a possible explanation is that the thunder in the rainy season is like a lion's roar.

This range of hills encircle Freetown, the capital of the colony, and to the north is the delta of the river. Westwards of the hills lies an extremely flat plain extending as far as the eye can see. The view from an aeroplane shows a network of creeks and marshes. To the north and south of the town are excellent bathing beaches, the ground on the extreme edges of the coast appearing to be of volcanic origin, although the colony is not in a zone of the earth's weakness.

Climate

The colony lies approximately between the equator and the Tropic of Cancer (9° - 13°) and consequently has, what I think is called, an equatorial climate. The seasons are not divided into hot and cold, but rather into wet and dry. The temperature remains approximately constant reaching its maximum around Christmas and is always extremely hot. The dry season extends from November to April and up country the two seasons are pretty well defined, but on the coast where we are situated, rains continue well into the dry season (at the time of writing there are still occasional showers), no doubt due to the hills. The days and nights are approximately equal, darkness descending suddenly about 18.30 and lasting until 07.00. At night the sky is nearly always illuminated by static disturbances. Up in the hills, where one finds the hospitals and the governor's residence are situated, the climate is more balanced and the heat and damp not so oppressive. No wonder Lady Astor on her visit, said that she thought the climate very nice and couldn't see why the troops were not kept out here three years instead of eighteen months! Needless to say she did not visit the delta where we are situated.

Population

The population consists principally of blacks, a small number of white administrators, a large number of forces and a small colony of Syrians who monopolise the trading.

The blacks can be divided roughly into coast dwellers and inland dwellers. The coast natives are mostly the descendants of liberated slaves who have been dumped here from the southern states. The societies for self-government all have sprung from this district. Personally, I have no doubt that if self-government were granted, the bulk of the natives would be worse off as the minority would certainly exploit their comrades. The cathedral is run by blacks, most of the public services are also native run e.g. police, railway, bus, postal. The natives who live up country were the original inhabitants, and are still run by chief and tribal law, the white district commissioner only suggesting what is to be done. He is also there of course to see that juju [a word used by Europeans to describe traditional West African religious practices] does not become too prevalent.

The white administrators are civil servants on whom the government of the colony really depends.

Forces consist mostly of Navy with a sprinkling of R.A.F. and R.W.A.F.F. (Royal West African Frontier Force) whose headquarters are in Nigeria.

No-one seems to know where the Syrians have come from but they have managed to monopolise the trade and exploit both black and white. Needless to say they are not popular.

Occupations and Industry

The colony is said to be very rich in minerals, but apart from a very little iron smelting no other industry is carried on. There is no coal and this is probably the reason of a lack of works.

The climate makes all agriculture very simple, the natives simply sowing and reaping without any thought of a crop failure. Rice, being the staple food of the native, is important. Tropical fruit and vegetables of all kinds are common.

One of the most important native occupations is the making of ornamental goods for sale to innocent white men. Crocodile bags, leopard skin bags, slippers, fans, knives, writing cases and many other things all very well made. When buying from a native he always asks about 3 times as much as he expects, and buying is quite an interesting game. Sometimes as much as forty minutes being taken to knock an object down from £1 to 5/-.

Communications

The Sierra Leone railway runs from Freetown for about 400 miles up country. It has 1st, 2nd and 3rd class compartments, the 3rd class being pretty poor. It has a very small gauge (about 2 ft), uses locomotives similar to those used at Monckton [the colliery where Norman's father and grandfather worked] and is staffed completely by natives.

Roads are fairly good and built mostly by the military authorities to military objectives. Air travel is slowly becoming important and the colony may soon become an important stepping stone in trans-continental travel. The river is used mainly by native craft but also by flying boats.

Religions

As may be expected Christianity in all its denominations has a strong hold. The Anglican Church having a bishop at Freetown and numerous mission churches. The Cathedral of St George is about 100 years old and possesses a very fine choir and organ. All its priests are natives and also the choir, wardens and so on.

Up country the natives still have their old superstitions and jujus. Devil women, snake gods, the changing of men into women and vice versa although scoffed at by whites are very real to the blacks and the witch doctor together with his bones and masks is an important figure in village life. Some of the natives are Mohammedans but I have come across no other beliefs."

Tuesday 4th January 1944

"Nothing very interesting all day.

Went to cinema and saw the American actress Alice Faye. For one who has seen nothing of white women for a long time this is a special treat. The sight of natives is interesting and amusing at first but soon pales. It is exactly 12 weeks to-night since I talked to a white girl on my last night at Dunfermline.

In a way it is good to come to a place like this and realise how good everything is that you normally despise.

Radio announces Russians within 1939 Polish frontier."

Wednesday 5th January 1944

"Again nothing to do.

While taking a P.D. in the morning noticed how perfectly camouflaged the crickets are. They look exactly like a piece of brown grass and only give their position away by their loud chirping. Like all the other insects, they are large being about four inches long.

The other day we uncovered a spider in a drawer almost as large as a saucer. Everything is big here due no doubt to the heat.

It is easy to imagine conditions in the primitive forests after having lived here. Opened a bottle of port at night left over from Xmas, but it is rank stuff and typical of all drink in this part of the world."

If P.D. stands for positive displacement, then it would have appealed to my dad's scatological sense of humour to use the term euphemistically for his visit to the latrines.

Thursday 6th January 1944

"Again nothing interesting to put down."

Friday 7th January 1944

"Great excitement during the night.

About 05.30 wakened by a terrific shout and awoke just in time to see a native dashing out of the door. Gave chase but could not catch him. It seems the seaman sleeping next to me, who is a very light sleeper, awoke and saw him in my locker. He immediately yelled but could not grab him owing to being impeded by his mosquito net. Petty thieving by natives is pretty bad. The man who was in my locker got away with a bar of toilet soap (highly prized by natives), a handkerchief and a few coppers."

Saturday 8th January 1944

"Went to cinema at night but not very good."

Sunday 9th January 1944

"Leading Hand of Guard."

In the Royal Navy the Leading Hand is the most senior of the junior ranks and is equal in status to a corporal. The insignia worn by leading hands is a single fouled anchor and on his photograph taken in 1943 Norman's badge can be seen on his left arm. In his photograph taken in 1945 he is wearing the insignia of Petty Officer on his left arm: crossed anchors with crown above.

Monday 10th January 1944

"Came off watch at 04.00.

Although I should have now got used to it, the tropical night still fascinates me.

The queer throbbing of the insects, the flashes of static disturbances in the sky, the queer glowing of the glow-worms (said to be calling its mate by means of light) all combine to make one realise how different it all is from the European night."

Tuesday 11th January 1944

"As these pages look rather blank I am going to fill them up with a précis of the chapter on the History of Sierra Leone from "The Gold Missus: A Female Prospector in Sierra Leone" by K Fowler-Lunn published in 1938.

Sierra Leone is the oldest of British African colonies, the territory around Freetown being purchased from a native prince at the end of the 17th century. But this is not the earliest history we know of Sierra Leone. As early as 500B.C. an expedition from Carthage, under Hanno, arrived at a large bay with mountains near it which has been identified as Freetown harbour. It is not known if he landed but he departed in haste after seeing the fires and hearing the drums and the cries of the natives ashore.

The French claim that Norman traders visited Sierra Leone and Upper Guinea in 1364 but this is disputed by the Portuguese who say they were the pioneers of West African trade.

At any rate, it is known that Henry the Navigator sent out an expedition in 1462 who claimed the country by right of discovery. References to the Portuguese language can still be found to-day. The Portuguese also introduced Christianity and the infamous traffic of slave trading. This latter practice was soon taken up by the English and in 1562, Sir John Hawkins carried away over 200 slaves to sell to the Spaniards. It seems that no-one attempted to colonise the place but just used it as a trading station.

In 1618 a company was formed in London and given land on the Cerbero river. Charles II gave it a royal charter and power to export 3,000 slaves annually to the British West Indies. It is estimated that between 1713 and 1733 more than 300,000 were exported.

It was 1785 before the French appeared but in that year they fortified two islands on the Sierra Leone River. In 1772 Mansfield had given his ruling that when a slave set foot in England he was automatically free. Many blacks who had served in the American Wars came to England, and, constituted a real problem until someone decided to return them to West Africa. Thus Freetown began.

After various troubles Sierra Leone became a Crown Colony on January 1st 1808. The crown colony consists of about 2,270 sq. miles on the coast. The rest of Sierra Leone was proclaimed a protectorate in 1896 in order to establish a boundary against the French encroachment on tribal territory. The language of the colony is pidgin English but the Protectorate still has tribal languages."

Friday 14th January 1944

"Heard this morning that an officer had been attacked in Freetown by natives, pepper being thrown into his face and followed by being beaten unconscious.

The natives seem to be getting a little out of hand and I would not be surprised if there wasn't a flare-up sooner or later.

A society flourishes in Freetown and all on the coast called the "Society of Young Africa" pledged to self-government who use these terrorist methods. The idea of them governing themselves is ridiculous, for one intellectual there are hundreds of illiterates and much more education is necessary.

They are already exploited by a gang of Syrian merchants who charge fantastic prices for their goods and the natives are too daft to leave them alone and trade with their own merchants."

Maybe "The Society of Young Africa" was associated with The West African Youth League founded in 1935 by Isaac T. A. Wallace Johnson. This was a political organisation opposed to colonial government in Sierra Leone and the Gold Coast (present day Ghana). In 1938 the League won council elections for the City Council in Freetown and Wallace Johnson claimed there were 40,000 members of the organisation. Resistance continued in the form of sporadic riots and strikes. Proposals were made in 1947 for a joint political system for both the colony and the protectorate. Astute politics by Sir Milton Margai managed to forge a consensus that resulted in a new constitution in 1951 and in 1953 Margai was elected as Chief Minister prior to a landslide majority in the first parliamentary elections in 1957. On 27th April 1961, Sierra Leone achieved independence from Britain and Sir Milton became the first Prime Minister. All appears to have gone well until his death in 1967 which heralded many years of military coups, one party state administrations, further failed attempts at democratic government, civil war and the intervention of over 10,000 United Nations peace-keeping forces before the British Army restored order after Operation Palliser in 2001. Subsequently the Truth and Reconciliation Commission and democratic presidential and parliamentary elections have been established in Sierra Leone.

Thursday 20th January 1944

"Spent all day in redecorating the billet in readiness for the coming of the Admiral on Sunday.

Distempered the inside cream and green and really made a good job of it.

The oranges' season is now well in and the crop is excellent. I was rather surprised to find oranges here as I seem to remember from Geog. lessons that they are a product of the Mediterranean climate but they do very well here.

Pineapples are also in and I had my first the other day. They are quite juicy but rather woody. I think I prefer the tinned variety."

Friday 21st January 1944

"It has not rained now for nearly two months and the country gets very dry and dusty. An interesting feature of the dry season is the coldness of the early mornings.

Since I arrived here I have worn nothing but a shirt and shorts, discarding the shirt later in the day but for these last few mornings underclothes and long trousers have been necessary and some chaps have even been dressing in European rig.

Later in the day the sun makes up for the coldness by being very hot indeed.

Fifteen weeks to-day since I left home."

Saturday 22nd January 1944

"Main event of the day was an E.N.S.A. concert at night.

It was even worse than usual. I keep saying that I will not go to another, but the lack of entertainment is so great that one would go mad if something to see at night did not turn up occasionally."

The Entertainments National Service Association or E.N.S.A. was an organization set up in 1939 by Basil Dean and Leslie Henson to provide entertainment for British armed forces personnel during World War II. Many well known stars performed in E.N.S.A. including Gracie Fields, George Formby, Wilfred Bramble and Vera Lynn. E.N.S.A. had to cover a vast area and despite large numbers of entertainers from both stage and screen it was spread thin on the ground. Consequently many entertainments were substandard and E.N.S.A. was widely regarded as standing for "Every Night Something Awful".

Sunday 23rd January 1944

"Great excitement caused by the visit of Rear Admiral Peters who has just taken over the West African Command."

Tuesday 25th January 1944

"4.45p.m. A partial eclipse of the sun stopped play in the L's and O's [perhaps Locals and Officers or Lower Ranks and Officers] cricket match. The sun was almost completely covered at the height of the eclipse and it was almost completely dark. I should imagine we had a better opportunity of seeing it than if we had been in England as here the sky is completely cloudless.

The natives were cowed by it and huddled together, and, although I am pretty sure they have some juju about it, I could not get anything out of them. They are always rather reticent about such matters."

Wednesday 26th January 1944

"Discovered more customs of the natives to-day.

Marriage takes place early, when the girls are between 12 and 14 years, and, before the ceremony the young bride-to-be is taken away from her parents and the clitoris is removed by means of elementary surgery.

The instrument used is an ebony knife.

Thus the women derive very little pleasure from sexual intercourse.

This takes place among the more primitive tribes, the Christians scorning such practice.

The man, for some unknown reason, has his hair shaved completely off for some weeks before the ceremony."

Thursday 27th January 1944

"Felt particularly bored to-night so four of us decided to break camp and go down to the "native".

This particularly appealed to us as we were doing something we ought not to do.

We got out successfully and a short walk brought us to the village. The pub is a mud and thatch shack with the front completely missing. A counter goes across it and the boozers sit on stools exactly like a milk bar. Behind the counter are shelves containing beer and wine.

As Treadway had visited here before we were invited into the back. This was an open courtyard with tables and benches and oil lanterns.

Reminded me rather of a Viennese beer garden.

The landlady's children waited on and brought bottles and glasses. As the beer cost 4/6 a pint we didn't indulge to our heart's content but enjoyed it nevertheless, possibly because we knew we were doing wrong.

Arrived back in camp safely without being caught."

Friday 28th January 1944

"Visited Freetown for the purpose of renewing library books.

I rather think that Freetown is now one of the largest overseas naval bases.

The harbour is ideal being one of the best in the world and, although I have no idea of the number of men around here, it must be pretty big.

Freetown is the base for the South Atlantic fleet and a pool of ratings is always kept in two luxury liners converted into naval vessels.

Although I have never been aboard either of them, I am told they are very grim as they are so overcrowded.

Incidentally, Spurwing has two functions - a squadron for anti-submarine work, and a storage depot for naval aircraft; so that a carrier coming in with its planes shot up, can remain in Freetown and be completely refitted from Spurwing.

During the last year only one carrier has ever needed this service - to my eyes this station is a typical waste of both material and man power."

This eerily reflects what Churchill had said to the First Lord of the Admiralty six months earlier when he had been railing about the huge cost of the Fleet Air Arm relative to its actual engagement with the enemy. In his typical, blunt manner he observed that out of 45,000 personnel only 30 had been killed, injured or taken prisoner in the previous three months! While expressing pleasure that so few had suffered and being at pains to attach no blame to either officers or men for the lack of activity, Churchill did warn the top brass that such a situation couldn't continue. Interestingly he was at the same time pushing ahead with the plans for the British Pacific Fleet where direct action on a huge scale was envisaged.

Sunday 30th January 1944

"Guard at 12.00.

A hectic time during the first watch owing to two sentries being adrift and having to root them out of the village."

Sunday 6th February 1944

Expedition to Marampa

"For a week or two now we have been anticipating this trip and when we awoke about 06.00 everyone was as happy as kids going to a Sunday School treat. Breakfast was soon disposed of and by seven we were on our way with all the food and drinking water stowed away. Drinking water had to be taken in old beer bottles because of the unhealthy water up country. Needless to say a few bottles of beer had been saved also from the week's ration.

When we set off the sun had not risen and the morning was extremely cold. On reaching the main road we turned in the opposite direction to Freetown. As the road has a very good surface we ran along at a good speed and consequently got colder and colder. The road ran up and down hills with monotonous regularity as we were skirting the foothills of the coast range and occasional sharp bends made us hold our breath. Luckily Spofford, a Yorkshireman from Bradford, is a good driver and we soon arrived at Waterloo.

Waterloo is an R.A.F. station and the end of the made up road. For thousands of miles, right across to East Africa, the population is nearly all black, with district commissioners separated by many miles of bush.

A hundred yards or so beyond Waterloo the road disappeared and a dusty cart track took its place. We had 65 miles still to do on a road hardly better than a country lane. The number of bends and corners increased and then to add to our difficulties we ran into a thick mist, which, as well as obscuring our view, deposited gallons of moisture on our clothes and soon put us all in a very miserable condition. The road was here running through a forest of palm trees with particularly dense undergrowth. We stopped here a minute or two and I, forgetting I had been sitting for nearly two hours, jumped out of the lorry and immediately fell flat on my face. However, apart from cutting my arms with the sword grass, I was unscathed and ate a hunk of dry bread which tasted very good. We then continued on our way.

As the forest thinned out so the mist disappeared and suddenly on rising over the top of a hill we saw a low, flat plain spread before us with the road twisting across it like a snake. In the distance a river gleamed in the early morning sun. The road got worse and, as the sun dried away the moisture, a cloud of red dust followed us and hung in the air for miles behind. Apart from a mud hut and a small hand dug field every few miles nothing interfered with the miles of eight and nine foot tall grass.

Eventually we arrived at the river and discovered to our great delight that there was no bridge; only a primitive ferry. It took it about 10 minutes to come across from the other side, the motive power being supplied by half a dozen natives and a primitive system of ropes and pulleys. While waiting we bought bananas and oranges at 3 a 1d and huge pineapples at 6d. The natives gathered round in numbers and stared at us all the time never having seen twenty white men at once for "many moons". When the ferry arrived we ran the lorry on and the pulling and tugging began again.

The dusty track seemed endless. At one of the small villages we found Sam, the orderly who was on leave and had walked there. We picked him up together with his son, two live fowls, a bag of beans and a sack of rice and continued. About 12.00 we arrived at the small iron mining town of Lunsar. This is a very small place, its only attraction being very cheap shopping. Silks at 3/6 a yd, bananas and oranges 3 a 1d, eggs 1/6 a dozen and straw baskets at correspondingly cheap prices. The mine is on a hill - the only hill for miles around and said to consist entirely of pure iron ore - and as I couldn't see any pit-head gear I assumed that it must be a dug hole.

We continued on our way and another six miles brought us to Marampa, a small village of a dozen huts but the home of the Paramount Chief of a section of the Mende tribe - one of the four great tribes of Sierra Leone. We bribed two court messengers - strapping fellows in red fezzes, black coats and brass buttons - to keep a curious crowd at a distance and had chop - bread, cheese, boiled eggs, sardines, tinned steak and kidney pudding and beer. We had intended paying our respects to the chief but unfortunately we were late and he had turned in for his afternoon nap, and, it appeared that it was more than anyone's life was worth to waken him, so we left him in peace and went back to Lunsar. Here we loaded the wagon up with eggs, dead ducks and chickens, fruit and cloths and silks; gave cigarettes and matches to everyone who looked important, said goodbye to a young beauty who wanted us to spend the night with her and by 15.00 we were on our way back.

The journey back was uneventful apart from a swim in the river while waiting for the ferry to come across - a welcome change from the sun and dust with water as warm as a bath - and we arrived back at Spurwing at approximately 18.15."

Today, Marampa is still the site of an iron ore mine near the town of Lunsar in Port Loko District. Lunsar is about fifty miles from Freetown, currently has a population of over 20,000 and is the main commercial centre of northern Sierra Leone. The iron ore forms part of a mountain called Massaboin Hill and it was first mined in 1933. It was mined until 1975 when falling global prices made it unprofitable; it was however re-opened in 2010. The opening ceremony was attended by government ministers, diplomats, company executives, state officials and local leaders including the Paramount Chief of Marampa.

Monday 7th February 1944

"Bathing in the afternoon.

Noticed on the road to Freetown a curious stone platform and discovered that it was the stone on which slaves were exhibited before being purchased.

Slavery was only finally stamped out in the colony about 1920 and is still known in the protectorate.

Actually I personally can see no difference between slavery and the purchase of wives which is still allowed.

Rather amused by a recruiting notice to West Africans stating that marriage allowances are only allowable on one wife."

Between 1530 and 1810, Britain and British ships played a major role in the transatlantic trade in captured Africans. Over ten million captured Africans were shipped to the islands of the Caribbean and to the Americas. Many more died during capture, while being marched to the coast, or in the appalling conditions of the slave ships. In 1807, the British Parliament passed the Slave Trade Act outlawing the practice and subsequently the Royal Navy operating out of Freetown took active steps to prevent the Atlantic slave trade.

Friday 11th February 1944

"Leading Hand of Guard.

Typical African night as always imagined in Hollywood.

Huge fires down in the village and all through the night the tom-toms and drums beat incessantly.

Moon rose about 22.30 and soon illuminated everything as bright as day."

Thursday 23rd March 1944

[It was Norman's 20th Birthday.]

Saturday 25th March 1944

"Why is it that one always begins a diary well but somehow it always peters out after the first few weeks?

However, a fresh start seems indicated so I'll try again.

A usual day, enlivened by being measured for concert party costumes in afternoon and the arrival of sea mail at night.

Birthday present from Mother only two days late."

Sunday 26th March 1944

"No transport so failed to go bathing to Lumley - first Sunday for some weeks now. Spent day reading month old newspapers."

Monday 27th March 1944

"Knocked off work at 11.00 and took up L.H.of G [Leading Hand of Guard], on afternoon watch.

Took my new recorder, sent by Mother, with me while walking between sentry boxes and practised scales. All the natives thought it great fun but I showed them that I wasn't quite daft and hadn't forgotten discipline by putting two in the rattle for being adrift.

Missed the Dogs and did the first and middle watches - the worst as the time drags so terribly."

The Rattle was a list of miscreants whose misdeeds would, in due course, be investigated by a senior officer. The Rattle was maintained by the Master-at-Arms, a Chief Petty Officer or Warrant Officer, responsible for discipline and adherence to the rules.

The Dog Watch is the naval name given to the work shift that takes place between 16.00 and 20.00. The period is split into two with the first Dog Watch being from 16.00 to 18.00 and the second, 18.00 to 20.00. It was introduced so that there could be some flexibility in allocating duties and also to create time for personnel to take an evening meal break. Following the Dog Watches the next watch, known as the First Watch is from 20.00 until midnight and the Middle Watch is from midnight until 04.00.

Tuesday 28th March 1944

"Stayed in bed until 12.00 recovering from the two watches.

Charlie brought me my breakfast to bed.

About the hottest day since we arrived here but clouds came over about 18.30 and a thunderstorm broke - the first rain, except for a small shower 29 Feb, since last December.

Lightning and thunder all night while we were at the cinema.

Film - "Above Suspicion" - a honeymoon couple spying in Germany. Plot revolves around the song "My Love is Like a Red, Red Rose" and the Liszt E Flat Piano Concerto.

Some good orchestra shots and a nice chunk of the concerto."

"Above Suspicion" was a 1943 MGM spy-drama starring Joan Crawford and Fred MacMurray.

Friday 31st March 1944

"Pay day and as the canteen had no beer went down to the village.

Three pubs had no beer but we managed to get a bottle at fourth one we tried.

All the matelots from the new transit camp at Robungba were there.

Rather disgusted to see a queue outside the native brothel, but I suppose every man does as he will with his own life.

Have noticed since joining the service that quite a number of men seem to forget their code of morals once they have left civilian life and this particularly takes effect when one comes to a place like Africa."

Saturday 1st April 1944

"Freetown in afternoon.

Nothing very special happening.

New law in operation stopping all members of H.M. Forces buying goods from civilian shops.

Hope it has been removed before I am due to go home.

Betty Grable at night in "Springtime in the Rockies".

Should have started drawing my tot but owing to late return from Freetown forgot all about it."

"Springtime in the Rockies" was a Twentieth Century Fox musical comedy film starring Betty Grable released in 1942.

Sunday 2nd April 1944

"Great event was my first tot.

I can almost reckon myself a real sailor now.

No noticeable after effects except an increased tendency to sweat."

It was a tradition in the Royal Navy to give everyone once they reached the age of twenty a daily glass of rum known as a "tot". The "tot" measures one eighth of a pint. The tradition started in 1655 and continued until 1970. The "tot" is still issued on special occasions following the order "splice the mainbrace". The order has to be given by the sovereign, a member of the royal family or in some circumstances a member of the Admiralty Board.

Monday 3rd April 1944

"Should have gone up in H.S. 463 on a Radar test but the damned thing developed transmitter trouble."

Aircraft operating from shore stations carried identification letters based on the actual name of the place. H.M.S. Spurwing was based at

Hastings (near Freetown) hence H.S. = Hastings although initially it had a single letter H.

"Worked on C.W. but not R/T [Radio Transmitter].

Dicky Treadway's 21st birthday.

Beer ration reduced to two pints a week but having some influence in the right quarter we managed to get extras.

However, not enough to make merry on but quite enough to make one forget Sierra Leone is such a __________place."

C.W. (so called after the Commission and Warrant Branch which organised it) was a scheme by which the lower ranks could apply to become an officer. During World War II those recruits who had signed up for the duration and who had educational qualifications were eligible to apply. The rank of Petty Officer was the lowest of the senior rates and it was a non-commissioned officer role. The route is clearly mapped out on Norman's "History Sheet for Radio Mechanics". After the Preliminary Training and Final (Service) Training the next step was "Recommendation for Petty Officer Radio Mechanic (A.R.) & (A.W.). A.R. was Air Radio and A.W. was Air Wireless. After that came "Recommendation for Chief Petty Officer Radio Mechanic" for which there was an examination.

Tuesday 4th April 1944

"Did not go to work as I was billet sentry.

Every day we take turns to keep watch over the billet to see that nothing gets pinched."

Wednesday 5th April 1944

"Went in H.S. 599 on Radar test with Dick doing a W/T [Wireless Telegraphy] test at the same time.

Felt some nasty quakes when the pilot went into a corkscrew dive over the harbour but otherwise unimportant.

Pleased to write that I am no longer troubled by air sickness."

Churchill had been personally involved in the development of radar right from the earliest days and he was very keen that the Royal Navy should make the most of its potential. In the 1930s, the possibility of using radio waves reflected back from aircraft and other metal objects had occurred to a number of scientists in Britain, the U.S.A., Germany and France. It was talked about as Radio Direction Finding (RDF) but later became known as "Radar". The practical aim was to be aware of the approach of hostile aircraft not by dependence on human observation but by the echo that was sent back from the radio waves. This was being actively developed in Great Britain by Professor Appleton after Professor Watson-Watt had, in February 1935, explained to a Parliamentary Committee that this might be feasible. At a meeting of the Air Defence Research Committee (A.D.R.C.) later in 1935 it was reported that early experiments had proved successful. A chain of stations were planned in the Dover - Orfordness area to experiment further. In July 1937 the A.D.R.C., under Churchill's leadership, approved plans to create a chain of twenty stations from the Isle of Wight to the Tees, to be ready by the end of 1939 at a cost of over one million pounds. Meanwhile further experiments were undertaken to transfer the technology to ships and to aircraft: although problems were encountered in aircraft at first because the size of the radio sets made them impracticable.

The need to identify who is on your side or who is the enemy -Identify Friend or Foe - has always been crucial in warfare and no more so than with aircraft. This need was becoming imperative at the same time as radar was developing. Early attempts were not very successful: one such was "Pipsqueak", a clockwork device that the pilot had to be constantly watching and which for fourteen seconds in every minute prevented radio transmission. In 1939 a new version known as I.F.F. (Identify Friend or Foe) Mark I was invented. This was a single unit comprising a receiver / transmitter carried in the aircraft that was to be identified. The I.F.F. was set into receive mode but when activated by a radar signal became a transmitter and returned a signal which could be recognised. These units operated on frequencies between 20 - 30 MHz. Norman was trained to work on I.F.F. Mark II (R3002/3, R3077/8 and R3108/9 being the codings in his service record) which operated on a much greater range of frequencies 40-50 and 60-70 MHz. He also trained for I.F.F. Mark III which was developed in order to accommodate the increasing use of radar and the need for a distinct frequency band for I.F.F. with a common equipment specification. The 157-187 MHz band was chosen and I.F.F. Mark III was a complete system including the transmitter, receiver, control boxes and coding units. Specifically he was trained to work on the Transponder (coded R3067/R3090 in his service record) which was a combined Receiver/Transmitter fitted to the unit aircraft which needed to be identified. Upon receipt of an interrogating signal it responded with a coded signal on the same frequency. The coding could be switched in form and duration for specific missions. The original British I.F.F. Mark III transponder (R3090) was copied in the U.S.A. for their naval aircraft so that eventually all the Allies were using the same equipment and frequencies.

Thursday 6th April 1944 (Maundy Thursday)

"Nothing to record all day except being measured for costumes in afternoon.

Went to confession at night with Lancaster.

Stayed talking until about 22.30 and then finished by saying Compline.

Nobody who has never been to confession can realise the immense feeling of joy and happiness one has after it."

Friday 7th April 1944 (Good Friday)

"Given the day off but as there was no church had nothing whatever to do.

Took up Leading Hand of Guard on the Dogs but as the transit camp ratings have taken over Guard duties nothing to do."

Sunday 9th April 1944 (Easter Sunday)

"Went to Grafton Pool in afternoon but did not go in."

Monday 10th April 1944 (Easter Monday)

"Holiday again to-day.

Stayed in bed until very late.

Went to New England (Combined R.N. and R.A.F. H.Q) to a fun fair.

Very disappointing as it consisted of rolling pennies, guessing peas etc. Left it and went to Freetown returning in time to catch lorry home.

Bishop of Freetown and wife present."

Tuesday 11th April 1944

"More light on juju.

Heard a story from a chap who has just come up from Kowenda, the Royal Navy air station on the Gold Coast, about a decision of the high and mighty to build a new hangar there.

They had decided on a spot and had started to build when the native witch doctor came and told them that they were building on the native chief's burial ground, and if they continued he would put a curse on the hangar ("flying bird house" he called it).

Of course, the contractors told him what he could do and continued with the work, but when it had just been finished it completely collapsed killing six men.

The story breaks down there as the hangar was re-built and is still there as far as I know, but skeletons had been found under the ground."

Friday 14th April 1944

"Should have been dress rehearsal for concert at night but when we arrived at the Robangba Theatre found it occupied by a crowd of pissed up R.A.F. chaps.

Great difficulty in clearing them out but finally succeeded but the whole action made us so late that we didn't finish until 23.30.

I think the whole thing is P.A.P. but the others are too thick skulled to see it."

"Pap" refers to an idea which lacks substance or value: drivel, balderdash or twaddle being synonymous. Maybe Norman wrote it like this to express his frustration with the progress of the show but judging by the photographs it looks as though it was hilarious.

Thursday 20th April 1944

"Again seem to have got a day or two behind.

Nothing much doing all day (as usual).

Should have been a rehearsal in afternoon. But no-one turned up. As the entertainments officer, who is compering the show, has gone up country, perhaps it will die a natural death. I hope so anyway.

Had a short downpour just before supper and had to don oilskins and topee. Rather strange that topees are supposed to be issued as protection against sun, but are never used when the sun is shining, only when it rains. They serve admirably as a preventative against raindrops down the neck.

Heard Mozart's G Minor at night. The opening bars always give me a thrill of pleasure. Definitely my favourite symphony."

The concert wasn't cancelled and Norman saved several photos of those who took part wearing their costumes.

The topee, otherwise known as a pith helmet, was often worn by Europeans in the tropics to shade the wearer's head and face from the sun. It was made of cork or pith (derived from an Indian swamp plant) in order to be light-weight and was covered in cloth.

Saturday 22nd April 1944

"A usual Saturday, enlivened by a display of tribal dancing at night.

Account of Tribal Dances given on "Spurwing" playing fields.

As we ambled across to the soccer pitch last night few of us had any idea of what was in store. Daily orders told us that dancers, acrobats etc. from all over West Africa were to appear. Since six o'clock lorries had been bringing the dancers from Freetown and they had spent the time in dressing up and practising the dances.

I can hardly begin to write about the night. A shower earlier in the day had removed all the clouds from the sky, and thousands of stars glittered from the great, black dome above. A slight breeze rustled the pale trees and a huge bonfire which had just been kindled threw light and shadow all over the field. On a dais at one side sat all the tribal chieftains in various coloured robes and the whole scene was illuminated by a great arc lamp used for night landings. About 8.30p.m. a soft beating on the tom-toms announced the beginning. From the opposite side of the arena a native band danced in with tom-toms and drums followed by about twenty young girls who swayed and swirled round to the rhythm. They were dressed in long silk robes which swirled in the dust, and, as the music quickened they danced all the harder until after about twenty five minutes of non-stop dancing a roll on the big drum finished the dance.

Next appeared a stilt dancer. With his legs fastened to ten foot long bamboo poles he presented a grotesque figure. First he danced in rhythm to the drums and then proceeded to give an amazing display of acrobatics on stilts, balancing on one stilt, bending over backwards and many other seemingly impossible feats. At the same time as the stilt dancer was performing two other chaps appeared, one who carried a torch and every so often shoved it into his mouth pretending to take a bite, and the other with a glass beer bottle in each hand from which he kept biting pieces of glass, chewing it and spitting it out again. As he did it blood ran out of his mouth in streams but this did not seem to deter him in the slightest. This continued for some time and then all three retired and a new band appeared on the scene. This consisted of hollowed out gourds filled with pebbles which sounded like babies rattles when played, tom-toms and a very elementary form of xylophone which was played by sticks.

Then into the arena came about ten girls with faces painted white, dressed only in a skirt with their breasts glistening in the firelight due to the application of some oil. They danced the first part of the Bundu ceremony – the only part which Europeans are allowed to see. The Bundu is a secret society for women and this ceremony is the one performed when the clitoris is removed in young girls as I have mentioned earlier. After this appeared yet another band and to a new rhythm appeared two Mendi devil dancers. They were dressed in a conical arrangement of straw which stretched from the neck downwards and made them look like hay ricks. They wore masks made of pieces of tinsel and glass which reflected the light and gave the impression that they were looking all over the place at the same time. They danced around for a while and almost immediately after finishing were followed by a conjuror. He had two tricks; one in which he pulled yards and yards of string from his mouth and the other in which he scooped water from the air and washed in it. Although they were both extremely elementary the natives were delighted and howled their approval.

The performance came to an end with first a troupe of mediocre acrobats followed by the "boneless babies" which proved to be three or four extremely agile kids with two natives to catch them in their acrobatic feat. Then all the natives who had appeared returned to the arena for a "grand finale" and made one hell of a noise before climbing into the lorries and returning to Freetown. The instruments used were mainly drums and tom-toms, an elementary xylophone, two one stringed fiddles and rattles. The sense of rhythm was extremely good, but I could not count one tune with more than seven notes and everything was in common time."

Carefully saved within the pages of the diary is the actual programme from the night which explains:

"Most village dances are held during the dry season after the rice harvest has been gathered. Dancers, drummers and acrobats are a lively feature at this time and drumming is heard far and wide over the countryside.

Dancing is generally a spare time recreation but there are many troupes of itinerant professionals who make their living by it. Most of the performers in this display are professionals.

Masked dancers play a prominent part in the ceremonies of the secret societies, of which the best known are the Porro for men and the Bundu for women. The objects and activities of these societies are a carefully guarded secret. Masked dancing is distributed over the whole of West Africa. A feature common to all is that no part of the performer's flesh must be visible. For a dancer to unmask in public was a serious offence.

The origin of stilt dancing is unknown. It is found in the north of Sierra Leone and in the Niger Delta and at a few places between.

Snake charmers are a close guild and the members have to undergo years of apprenticeship and training which is carried out in seclusion."

The programme lists all the names of the tribes and the Headman of each tribe in Freetown.

Monday 12th June 1944

Norman's service record shows that he was promoted to the rank of A/P.O.RM (AR)TY - Acting Petty Officer Radio Mechanic (Air Radio) Temporary.

He made no further entries in his diary in relation to his service at H.M.S. Spurwing.

Between 1st November - 18th December 1944 Norman's service record attaches him to H.M.S. Daedalus which was the Fleet Air Arm Headquarters at Lee-on-Solent and during much of this period he was in transit on his way home to the UK.

H.M.S. Spurwing at Hastings (near Freetown), Sierra Leone was decommissioned at the end of December 1944.

Thursday 16th November 1944 Return to UK

"When we got up this morning, what a sight - the snow covered hills around the Clyde. Dropped anchor in Greenock 09.00 hrs.

Left by lighter in afternoon.

Took train for London in late afternoon."

Friday 17th November 1944

"Arrived at R.N. Barracks Lee-on-Solent 16.00 hrs."

Saturday 18th November 1944

"Went on 15 days F.S. [Foreign Service] Leave."

Sunday 19th November 1944

"Arrived home."

19th December 1944 - 7th March 1945 Further training in the U.K

After his leave Norman was based at H.M.S. Waxwing, the transit camp in Scotland where he'd been based before his posting to Sierra Leone. He was there for a couple of weeks before attending further training at H.M.S. Gosling at Warrington. In addition to basic training for recruits, this base also provided specialist training for air fitters and air mechanics and for those working on electronics, radar and radio. There was also a facility to convert vehicles for use with mobile radio and radar. The men were kitted out for the tropics and the training included morale boosting talks plus commando style training in jungle fighting, self defence and survival.

Embarkation on R.M.S. (Royal Merchant Ship) Empress of Scotland was next.

Friday 9th March 1945

"I get back. Spent the evening leaning over the rail and watching the lights of Liverpool. How I should have liked to have been ashore."

Saturday 10th March 1945 Off to Sea again

"Left England. A pathetic party of girls from the dockers' canteen sang songs as we left the dock trying to cheer us up. By Hell, but I felt terrible watching England slip away once again."

The Empress of Scotland was a beautiful liner built in 1929 by Fairfield Shipbuilding at Govan on the Clyde in Scotland. Originally known as The Empress of Japan, on conversion to a troop carrier her name had been changed on the special orders of Winston Churchill as it was against regulations to change a ship's name in war-time. However, the irony of the original name wasn't lost on anyone.

A high level of secrecy had surrounded the mission and the personnel were not informed until they were on their way to Sidney, Australia that they were enroute to join the British Pacific Fleet which was already at war with the Japanese.

The war in Europe was moving rapidly towards its conclusion and the war in the Pacific was not regarded as particularly relevant by the British public or indeed Britain's serving men and women. The Government propaganda machine had to work hard to persuade people to support the Pacific War. They needed to convince the public that the war against the Japanese was just as much part of the struggle as the war against Germany, and that Japan was as culpable as Germany had been. The message that this was a war for freedom both at home and in the Dominions had also to be promoted along with the sense of Britain's obligation towards the Dominions because of their huge contribution to the war effort. Because of the impression in the country that the Pacific war was just America's war, the propagandists needed to make the public realise that Britain's future prosperity depended on reclaiming territory and regaining access to raw materials. Within the Royal Navy, a full programme of education and propaganda was undertaken to try to generate commitment to the next stage of the war which Churchill and his advisers envisaged would last throughout 1946 and well into 1947.

Politically, in order to maintain Britain's position on the international stage, it was seen as important for it to be part of the coalition that would end the war with the Japanese but the balance of power had completely changed and the United States of America was now the dominant partner.

Because of political sensitivities, it was imperative that the Royal Navy be self reliant in the Pacific and since mid-1944 plans had been in development to establish a Fleet Train to ensure adequate and continuous supplies, support and re-fuelling across the 12,000 miles from Britain to Australia. There was a determination by the British

Government that as the surrender of Germany became inevitable the best of what remained of the British Fleet would be sent out into the Pacific.

Traditionally, the Royal Navy had maintained a network of bases all over the globe for fuel, ammunition, spare parts, maintenance and the accommodation of men who were either in transit or whose ships were being re-fitted. Ships operated within range of their base and returned as necessary. For the British Pacific Fleet the Royal Navy would have to rely on support in Dominion countries; and the United States of America would also be providing much of the resources that the British Pacific Fleet needed to function in the struggle. The speed of the American advance meant that time was of the essence.

To provide repair, maintenance and servicing for the aircraft which would be needed by the ships of the British Pacific Fleet, ten self-contained Mobile Naval Operating Air Bases (MONABs) were planned.

Each MONAB was made up of several key components which were common to all units and provided the equipment and trained personnel needed to run an air base. These were a Commanding Officer; an administrative department responsible for medical matters, sanitation, wages, stores, clothing, catering, maintenance, accommodation and transport; an aircraft repairs and maintenance section; an operational and training section and a defence section. In addition there were a range of inter-changeable technical components. Each technical component carried out a single function such as day-to-day servicing, aircraft storage, repair of damaged aircraft etc. Should the MONABs duties be changed additional components could be added to meet the new task; alternately, redundant components could be removed or re-deployed.

On 24th August 1944, the Admiralty commissioned a disused R.A.F. airfield at Ludham, in Norfolk, as MONAB Headquarters to be known as H.M.S. Flycatcher. It was intended that MONAB personnel would be assembled and trained here. The first MONAB sailed in November 1944 arriving in Sidney, Australia on 18th December 1944. It encamped in tents at Warwick Farm Racecourse aka H.M.S. Golden Hind in the suburbs of Sidney. Stores had been packed up and loaded in a rush and as they were unloaded in a similar manner chaos ensued; labelling was muddled and mismatched; packed up in a wet English autumn many of the supplies and parts arrived corroded. However by mid-January 1945 order was returned; a new base was set up known as H.M.S. Nabbington and MONAB 1 stopped being mobile and began to function just like a large air station in the U.K.

The plan was that there would be ten MONABs in total. Each MONAB was given an H.M.S. name that began with "Nab" to reflect the NAB in MONAB. Norman was attached to MONAB 4. All the war-time MONABs were based in or near Sidney or Brisbane in Australia. The exception was MONAB 4 which was to be based in the Admiralty Islands over two thousand miles from Australia in the Pacific Ocean. Norman and his colleagues in MONAB 4 certainly drew the short straw.

MONAB 4 was assembled at Ludham on New Year's Day 1945 under the command of Captain A.N.C. Bingley. The ship's personnel were embarked in the S.S. Dominion Monarch and the stores and equipment in the S.S. Clan Macauley. They departed for Sidney, New South Wales, Australia on January 16th 1945. While the men were in transit the planning staff at British Pacific Fleet headquarters decided that MONAB 4 would become the first unit to be established in the forward area and, although too late to re-direct the men, the stores ship was sent straight to the Fleet anchorage at Manus, Admiralty Islands. Its operational base was to be at Ponam Island, near Manus, where U.S. Navy airfield facilities had been loaned from the Americans. An advance party was flown out to unload and fortunately the Americans stayed on to help. The Royal Navy air base at Ponam was commissioned as H.M.S. Nabaron (MONAB 4) on 2nd April 1945 and was the most northerly of all the wartime MONABs. In addition to its primary role of supporting disembarked front line squadrons, H.M.S. Nabaron (MONAB 4) was also tasked with providing reserve aircraft storage, repair and maintenance.

Norman was attached to a technical component: Maintenance, Storage & Reserve 6 (M.S.R.6) which was sent to join H.M.S. Nabaron (MONAB 4) a few weeks after the initial departure. M.S.R.6 was tasked with maintaining and storing reserve aircraft. It was attached to H.M.S. Nabaron (MONAB 4) where reserve aircraft stocks were held for either local issue or onward progress to the action zone. Individual M.S.R. units were attached to specific different aircraft types and M.S.R.6 specialised in Firefly, Seafire (the naval version of the Spitfire) and Sea Otter aircraft. An M.S.R. unit had its own complement of 3 Officers, 29 Petty Officers and 99 ratings which was how Norman came to be embarked on R.M.S. Empress of Scotland in March 1945 en-route for Australia.

Friday 16th March 1945

"Still at sea. However people can write poetry and extol the sea I don't know. I hate the sight of it.

Am spending my time at present in reading. There are innumerable paper-backed books on board and I read on an average one a day. To-day it was "English Diaries 19th Century". I particularly liked the selections from Dorothy Wordsworth's."

Tuesday 20th March 1945

"Eleventh day at sea. Well into the tropics now. Sun extremely hot and most of us suffering from sunburn to some degree.

For the past few days we have been passing great patches of bright red sea-weed which makes one presume that we are somewhere near the Caribbean or Saragossa sea. Passed several islands this morning which must have been part of the West Indies.

Expect to arrive at Panama any day now.

Still passing my time by copious reading - the last few days being devoted to "Claudius the God" by Robert Graves; a very interesting historical novel of the reign of Claudius Caesar. One paragraph which intrigued me was the trial of Messalina, Caesar's wife, where it was proved that she challenged a common prostitute to a competition to see which of them could have the most number of intercourses. The prostitute was finished after twenty five but Messalina continued well above this figure almost until dinner time the next day."

Saturday 24th March 1945

"Again I pick up my pen to record the happenings of the last few days.

Early on Thursday morning we sighted land and soon arrived at Christobel, the seaport on the Atlantic side of the Panama Canal, where we moored all day. The docks are particularly clean but this is not surprising as they are not used for heavy cargoes. Went ashore in the afternoon but only in the dock area. All the roads are lined with avenues of palm trees which give a pleasant shade. The Canal Zone, as it is called, is, of course, owned by the U.S.A. although situated in the republic of Panama and all the administration is done by the U.S. government. They are very efficient too. At night the U.S.O. (the U.S. Forces entertainments organisation) gave us a concert which was very good and afterwards the American Red Cross gave us books, ice-cream, cookies and fruit to come back on board with which I thought was very good of them. There is no doubt that the U.S. looks after its armed forces much better than the British do.

Early on Friday morning we were on the move again and soon were in the Canal proper. The first miles or so are uneventful as they pass through the reclaimed swamp-land; then one arrives at the first of three locks. These are massive constructions and easily take a ship of this size (650 ft long). The lock takes approximately 15 minutes to fill or empty and one can almost watch the water level rising. The ship is manoeuvred by small electric engines (2 forward and aft to port and starboard) which make the whole operation look like child's play. When the Canal was first attempted the idea was to cut straight through and unite the Atlantic and the Pacific, but the attempt was a failure due to the fact that the ground rises and also to the prevalence of malaria and yellow fever. Ferdinand de Lesseps original cutting can be seen just before the first locks are reached. When the Yanks took over they first drained the marshes so removing the disease by taking away the mosquitoes breeding grounds and then began cutting and constructing the locks.

After the first three locks which all raise the ship, one runs into a fresh water lake - Lake Gatun. This is quite large and is studded with numerous islands all of which are covered with exotic tropical foliage. As the salt water showers were now pumping fresh water most of us took the opportunity to have a good wash. The shores were also covered in foliage and the hills in the background made a beautiful picture. The canal then flows through a gorge cut out of the rock. Work is still progressing in this section. Then after more locks, very similar to the previous ones in shape which lowered the ship, we arrived at Bilboa, the port on the Pacific side and soon we were out to sea again. By nightfall land was out of sight. Needless to say the Canal is very well patrolled by armed guards and guards patrolled the ship all the time.

Today has not been exceptional. Began reading "Moon and Sixpence" a novel by Somerset Maugham based on the life of Paul Gauguin but don't feel qualified to give an opinion of it yet. Dukas' "Sorcerer's Apprentice" played during gramophone time. Like it very much especially the "pom-pom" bit where the broom comes to life. Also "Hold Tight" by Louis Armstrong.

Friday was also my birthday, my twenty first. What a place to come of age - a dirty great troopship with nothing to drink but orange juice and nowhere to go and have a good time!!"

By March 1945 much of the British Pacific Fleet was assembled at Manus in the Admiralty Islands. Initially it had been decided to base the British Pacific Fleet at Sidney in Australia but the logistics of the Fleet Train presented a huge challenge because of the considerable further distance from Australia to the theatre of war and it was quickly realised that an intermediate base was needed as well. The Americans agreed that their base at Manus which had been their main base for the re-capture of the Philippines could be used. By the end of 1944 the U.S. Navy had moved on thus creating much needed space and facilities for the British Pacific Fleet at Manus. An entry in the official naval diaries of the day records that Manus possessed a most objectionable climate which rarely improved at any time of year and the writer wryly speculates as to the sense of humour of whoever named the "unpleasant" islands after their Lordships at the Admiralty. At

Manus there was a large natural harbour which had been enhanced by the addition of three floating docks, stores depots and repair facilities. Air stations had been constructed by American SeaBees (C.B's - Construction Battalions) on the nearby islands of Pityilu and Ponam. Even so it was still a further 700 miles from Manus to the combat area.

The Americans had already attacked Iwo Jima on 19th February 1945 and after a long struggle lasting over a month achieved victory. The British Fleet, known as Task Force 57, comprising the battleships H.M.S. King George V and H.M.S. Howe plus four carriers with 250 aircraft, five cruisers and eleven destroyers left Manus on 18th March 1945. It reached its battle area east of Formosa on March 26th. It was the largest British Royal Navy force ever assembled in history and it was charged with invading Japan and re-gaining Malaysia.

Meanwhile, Norman was still in transit somewhere in the Pacific Ocean en route to Sidney, Australia.

Evening of 25th/26th March 1945

"Crossed the Equator for the first time in my life."

The Crossing the Line ceremony was for all those who were going into the southern hemisphere for the first time. Rituals involving shaving foam and being thrown into a tank of salt water were part of the traditions of this ceremony going back for decades.

Norman was an accomplished pianist and had a great love of classical music. In the summer before he joined the Fleet Air Arm he attended a Workers' Educational Association (W.E.A.) Summer School at one of the colleges of Cambridge University to study musical appreciation. His interest in music explains the content of the next three diary entries. How there came to be such a various collection of gramophone records on board The Empress of Scotland is a matter of conjecture but clearly there were others on board who enjoyed classical music as much as Norman did.

"Gramophone Recital on board Empress of Scotland 31.3.45

Overture "Oberon" Weber

"Italian Caprice" Tchaikovsky (Like it very much. Worth getting.)

Toccata and Fugue in D minor Bach

"Jesu, Joy of Man's Desiring" Bach

Ballade in A flat major Chopin

Scherzo - Concerto Symphonique Litoff

Concerto Grosse in B flat major Handel (Well worth getting. Leon Goosens on the oboe).

Symphony No 5 (Scherzo and Finale) Beethoven

Overture "Barber of Seville" Rossini

March - "Damnation of Faust" Berlioz

Excerpt from Act 3 "Die Meistersingers" Wagner (Walther's Prize Song)"

Sunday 1st April 1945 Easter Day

"Went to Mass in morning.

Nothing much to put in re the last week as we have been at sea all time.

Every day more or less the same.

Church Maundy Thursday and Good Friday.

Also a gramophone recital of "Messiah" on Good Friday. My recording with Mariel Brunsbill, Dora Laherte, Hubert Eisdale and Harold Williams.

Gramophone recital 3/4/45

Pomp and Circumstance No 1 Elgar

Overture "Rosamunde" Schubert

Waltz "Eugene Onegin" Tchaikovsky

Bolero Ravel

Valse Triste Sibelius

T&F. in D Minor (once again) Bach

Caprice Kriesler

Overture "Romeo and Juliet" Tchaikovsky".

Wednesday 4th April 1945

"Again nothing much to note except the amazing fact that when I go to bed to-night I shall wake up on Friday morning. This is not due to the fact that I'm particularly tired but that owing to crossing the International Date Line we miss a complete day. We have been retarding the clock an hour almost every other day and are now eleven hours behind G.M.T. [Greenwich Mean Time]. When we retard it another hour to-night and jump tomorrow we shall be twelve hours in front of G.M.T."

Saturday 7th April 1945

"How quickly this week has gone as we missed out Thursday.

Amazing display of phosphorescent fireworks on spray tonight. Lights up whole side of ship.

Expect to arrive a.m. Mon."

Monday 9th April – Saturday 26th May Sidney, Australia

"Once more this journal has been put away so the best thing I can do is give a general account of events since the last entry.

On the morning of the 9th April we arrived at Sydney, largest city in Australia and second largest in British Empire. Before entering the great harbour the sea was very choppy but once inside became calm and we moved alongside without incident. The main impression I now recall is the first view of the magnificent bridge across the harbour.

About the middle of the afternoon we disembarked and travelled to a Naval Air Station a few miles outside the city which was to be our home for the next few weeks. We settled down and that same night caught the electric train back into the city. Our first call was an eating house (American style with little alcoves for couples) where we made up for the bad food on the ship with steak, eggs and chips. Sydney seems to be full of these houses and also milk bars. Its trams, trains, etc are very antiquated. It seems to be a city of ancient and modern all mixed up.

After the big eats we walked around for a while and finding that all the pubs close at 6p.m. had to go to the Fleet canteen for a drink. This place proved to be full of drunken matelots so we did not waste any time there but went instead to a film. The prices were quite reasonable and the building was very modern having comfortable seats and concealed lighting, but the film itself was very old. We were to find that all the shows out here were very much behind England - some of them I had seen at Royston before leaving home.

Afterwards we ate again and made our way to Central Station which is about the size of Leeds City [Station]. Here we caught a train, but, unfortunately, it proved to be the wrong one and after going to its terminus had to come all the way back and catch the right one. Wc got back to camp about 4a.m. and it was bitterly cold, found that we had no beds and shivered until 6.30.

The following afternoon, having been given it off, we again went into Sydney. The shops were open and some of them are very big indeed. There are quite a few big departmental stores like Lewis's and most of the 6d stores are here. We found our way to the "British Centre", a big building where the servicemen can get cheap food, recreation, information etc. but after eating did not feel like having organised entertainment so went to get a closer view of the bridge. Took a tram to the harbour and then mounted many steps up to the bridge and walked across it. The view is grand and the height above water amazing. Returned and had tea and at night went to Luna Park. This is the Blackpool Pleasure beach of Sydney but is not very good so soon left it.

The days passed quickly. We went to shows, saw the Sydney Symphony Orchestra, met Mrs Mellors' niece, Shirley, ate many, many steaks, eggs, ice-creams, milk shakes, apples, grapes, etc and went for a day to Katoomba in the Blue Mountains. Just before leaving Sydney spent five days up there."

The British Centre had been set up to provide facilities for servicemen on leave. It could offer canteen facilities and 1,800 beds for overnight stays. With 13,500 men on shore leave on any one night facilities were stretched. However Australian families opened up their homes and offered meals and friendship to thousands of men who were so far away from home. Maybe that's how Norman had come to meet Mrs Mellors and Shirley.

The Blue Mountains are situated about thirty miles to the west of Sidney and extend for almost four thousand square miles. The area consists mainly of a sandstone plateau dissected by many deep gorges. The highest point is almost 4,000 feet above sea level. Since 2000, many parts of the Blue Mountains have been designated as a World Heritage Site.

"On Tuesday 8th May the newspapers were head-lined "It's all over in Europe" and gave histories of the last five years. Flags were flying in Sydney but no crowds surged through the streets. We made sure our rooms were booked at the British Centre and went for a drink to celebrate Victory. A couple of drunken sailors were the only signs of the momentous day it was. At seven o'clock we were steaming out of Central Station just as the city began to warm up and celebrate.

Australian trains are horrible. They are uncomfortable, slow, draughty and Heaven knows what else, in fact not a patch on the good old L.M.S. [London, Midland and Scottish Railway.] The only interesting part of the journey was an old man of 83 who got on at Penorth and who had emigrated here when he was 19. He had many interesting stories of the old days.

Arrived at Katoomba, highest point in the Blue Mountains about 10p.m. and after eating - the inevitable steak - got to our hotel just in time to hear Churchill's speech. Soon we were in bed, well wrapped up as this is very much colder than Sydney.

The next few days were grand and it was not pleasant to come back on the following Saturday. The next week passed quickly and, apart from a piano recital and a violin recital (Bach's E Major Partita and a Beethoven Sonata Op. 12 No. 1) was nothing momentous.

On Saturday 19th May 1945 we left Bankstown and joined H.M.S. Arbiter, an escort carrier. Tuesday saw us in Brisbane where we went ashore but did not like it much and as I write we are "somewhere at sea" sweating and looking forward to seeing "terra firma" once again."

During his stay in Sidney, Norman was attached to H.M.S. Golden Hind, a transit camp built on the racecourse in the outskirts of Sidney. Whether or not he did any work while in Sidney is a matter of conjecture. Reading his diary, it doesn't sound like it but at the time the other MONABs were working flat out to get the supplies, fuel and aircraft sorted and forwarded to the main British Pacific Fleet base at Manus.

H.M.S. Arbiter was an escort carrier built in the U.S.A. and given to the Royal Navy as part of the Lend-Lease scheme. After several Atlantic runs transporting Lend-Lease aircraft and ammunition, passengers and personnel, Arbiter was sent to Harland and Wolff's shipyard in Belfast for a "tropicalisation" re-fit. In February she embarked twenty four Corsair IVs of 1843 Squadron and began to prepare for passage to Australia, sailing on March 1st 1945 via Gibraltar, Port Said, Suez Canal, Colombo, Ceylon (now Sri Lanka) and arriving at Sidney, New South Wales, Australia on May 1st. More aircraft and personnel, including Norman's unit M.S.R.6, joined Arbiter before she sailed for the British Pacific Fleet anchorage at Manus, Admiralty Islands. Four days out she hit a typhoon and it was only because the tanks full of fuel acted as ballast that she didn't keel over. Finally Arbiter sailed on to Ponam Island where M.S.R.6 finally caught up with MONAB 4.

Saturday 2nd June 1945 Admiralty Islands (British Pacific Fleet)

"Last Monday saw us drop anchor in the Admiralty Islands at Manus. This is quite an extensive tropical island with a fairly high range of hills. Twice we went ashore to a small island in the bay for bathing. We also had a ration of one bottle of beer which by a little wangling grew into three. This was the first time I'd ever been ashore in a real liberty boat. [Traditionally "liberty boats" were the ship's boats that carried sailors ashore in foreign ports: so called because they freed the men at last after months of hard work and iron discipline.]

The heat below decks is terrific - one only has to take a cup of tea in the P.O's [Petty Officers'] mess and sweat pores out of you. Fortunately, the beauty of tropical mornings and evenings make up for a lot.

Yesterday we weighed anchor in the morning and a few hours sailing brought us to Ponam, a small island just off the main one, two miles long by six hundred yards wide. Highest point above sea level 6 ft. About 12.00 we came ashore in the cutter and surveyed our new home.

To look at it is a typical desert island complete with lagoon, coral and wind swept palm trees. Vegetation found growing naturally appears to be coconut palms, wild orange trees, bread fruit with a few tropical flowers and grasses. The seasons appear to be two - wet and dry. (Now we are at the end of the wet). Rainstorms are fairly common. The main island of Manus lies about a mile across the straits and is fairly large. I judged it at some ten miles long; the ground rises to a range of hills between 2,000ft and 3,000 ft and the whole is covered with vegetation. Sea life so far seen consists of small fish, coral snakes, small octopus and hermit crabs. The latter are small crabs which find an empty shell and carry it around with them, discarding them at successive intervals."

Norman didn't write any more accounts in his diary. He told a relative that all the men expected to be involved in hand to hand fighting and to die; he said they tried to be drunk as much as possible. On the island they worked from dawn to dusk with little for entertainment although there was an open air cinema built by the American SeaBees when they had initially established the base at Ponam. By June 1945 the 1,108 men who were stationed at Ponam with very little to spend their money on had accumulated over £20,000 in their branch of the Post Office Savings Bank. (About £500,000 in present day money.)

From the air Ponam Island looked rather like an aircraft carrier and the American SeaBees had built an airfield on it using crushed coral for the runway. The island was handed over to the Royal Navy fully equipped.

As well as the airstrip there were aircraft repair shops and storage for aircraft parts; petrol and oil storage tanks; a control tower; jeeps and trucks; huts for accommodation and an officers' mess; dining halls; a hospital; a water de-salination plant and kitchens. (The kitchens even included an ice-cream maker). The U.S. Navy also left behind a forty strong team of SeaBees personnel to maintain the island and its facilities.

H.M.S. Nabaron (MONAB 4) had been built up rapidly to ensure an accessible supply of aircraft for the British Pacific Fleet. Its primary task was to maintain a pool of operational aircraft in a serviceable state of readiness which were also available for replacement aircrew to fly when they arrived at the base and so help them keep in practice. It was also a training base for air gunners and several target towing aircraft were maintained for gunnery practice. The ship's company included electronics and communications specialists; radio technicians; armourers (maintainers and repairers of small arms and weapons systems); fitters (users of machine tools to make or modify parts); riggers (specialists in moving and lifting extremely large or heavy objects) and skilled mechanics.

H.M.S. Nabaron (MONAB 4) had its own newspaper "The Jungle Echo" which was printed out on paper provided by the U.S. Navy. On 29/4/45 it had reported the bombing of Manus by a single, lone Japanese aircraft at two o'clock in the morning.

Norman's unit M.S.R.6 was attached to H.M.S. Nabaron (MONAB 4) primarily for support of the Firefly I, Seafire III and Sea Otter aircraft of 1701 squadron but there is a photograph of a line of Corsairs in his photograph collection that suggests he may have had some involvement with these aircraft too. Through the Lend-Lease arrangements with the U.S., the Royal Navy had large numbers of American Wildcats, Hellcats, Corsairs and Avenger aircraft to complement its own planes.

The campaign to take Okinawa was still underway only reaching a conclusion on June 22nd 1945. A Japanese garrison of just over 100,000 had fought the American divisions of 450,000 men. The Japanese fleet had been virtually wiped out. Thirty four Allied destroyers and two hundred other Allied craft had been hit or sunk by 1,900 Kamikaze suicide bombers. The British Pacific Fleet had continued in action until April 20th 1945 with the Fleet re-fuelling at sea until exhaustion of supplies and heavy damage to aircraft forced a temporary retreat to Leyte in the Philippines. The British Pacific Fleet had sailed out again from Leyte on May 1st and for the next three weeks bombarded the island of Miyako. The carriers Formidable and Victorious were badly damaged by suicide bombers but were able to carry on until May 25th when, with supplies running low, the Fleet withdrew to Manus Island causing Admiral Spruance of the U.S. Navy to congratulate their efforts appreciating their fine work and co-operative spirit. The invasion of Japan was planned for September 1945. It was intended to attack the Japanese mainland, sink what remained of Japanese ships and wreck Japanese airfields. In addition it would be necessary to find and destroy 4,000 aircraft hidden in the Japanese countryside each one with an expert pilot prepared to undertake kamikaze. According to Churchill, one million armed Japanese were willing to die for their country. Once it was clear that Okinawa would be captured American General Marshall offered the British a base there for ten squadrons that would take part in the air bombardment of Japan.

On Friday July 20th 1945 "The Pacific Post: Daily Newspaper of the British Pacific Fleet" was launched. Norman kept a copy of the first edition with his diary. The lead story was headlined:

"Air Strike at Jap's Hidden Fleet"

It reported that Allied planes had swept down over Tokyo Bay the previous day and attacked the remnants of the Japanese Fleet hiding in Yokosuku naval base. These ships had remained under camouflage since their defeat in the Philippines in October 1944. Five hundred planes had taken part in this and other attacks on Tokyo airfields and military establishments. Admiral Nimitz (Commander in Chief of the United States Pacific Fleet) had confirmed the raids but said that accurate reconnaissance of damage was prevented by adverse weather. Tokyo Radio had admitted that one thousand civilians were killed and wounded in the shelling. The great majority of Tokyo residents were living in underground shelters, preferring to stay there rather than move elsewhere.

Thursday 26th July 1945

A demand for an unconditional surrender was made by the President of the U.S.A., the President of the National Government of the

Republic of China and the Prime Minister of Great Britain on behalf of their millions of countrymen but was rejected by the military rulers of Japan.

Monday 6th August 1945

An American B29 bomber "Enola Gay" dropped a nuclear weapon known as "Little Boy" on the Japanese city of Hiroshima. It caused 120,000 civilian deaths. All wooden structures in a 1.2 mile radius were destroyed. 2/3 of all buildings in the same radius were destroyed. Meanwhile the conventional airstrikes continued.

Thursday 9th August 1945

A nuclear bomb known as "Fat Man" was dropped on the Japanese city of Nagasaki killing 74,000 people and injuring 74,000 more. At the same time, the Japanese Supreme War Council was meeting to discuss terms of surrender because the Soviet Union had now also declared war on Japan.

H.M.S. Indefatigable and other R.N. ships continued strikes on airfields, installations and coastal shipping as did the U.S. Navy.

Wednesday 15th August 1945

The Japanese military leaders surrendered unconditionally.

Sunday 2nd September 1945

The formal surrender to the Allied commanders by the Japanese leadership took place on U.S.S. Missouri.

Wednesday 26th September 1945

Captain Bingley, Norman's Commanding Officer, had become ill and was taken back to Sidney, Australia for treatment. He was not able to return to duty and his place was taken by Captain C.J. Blake. Captain Blake had been ordered to place H.M.S. Nabaron (MONAB 4) on one month's notice to close down. Personnel were informed that the air station was to be taken out of service. On 26 September 1945 the first part of H.M.S. Nabaron (MONAB 4) to be stood down and embarked on H.M.S. Vindex bound for Australia was Maintenance Storage and Reserve Unit 6 (M.S.R. 6) - Norman's unit. H.M.S. Vindex had already embarked several hundred servicemen who had been Prisoners of War of the Japanese before stopping at Ponam to pick up more servicemen bound for home.

Gradually other elements of H.M.S. Nabaron (MONAB 4) were dispersed with the final handover of Ponam Island back to the Americans on 31st October 1945. Capt. Blake wrote in "The Jungle Echo" for the last time recording how impressed he was by the manner in which all the men had worked in harmony with each other while still retaining their individuality and urging the men to take the Nabaron spirit with them into their future lives.

The experience of H.M.S. Nabaron (MONAB 4) at Ponam can easily give a false idea of the effectiveness of a MONAB in the tropics because everything had been made simpler and the functioning of the Air Station made more efficient by the use of American equipment. Because of the semi-permanence of the facilities at Ponam, H.M.S. Nabaron became less a Mobile Air Base and more and more a Naval Air Station. Much of the gear brought out from England remained unused, notably tents for accommodation, generators for power and lighting and galleys. It had not been anticipated that some of the equipment left by the Americans such as heavy lifting cranes, machines for making and maintaining roads and air strips, refrigerators, a parachute packing room with a dehumidifier and a host of other items would even be needed. Official reports written by the commanding officer stressed that without these extras life would not only have been more arduous, but the station could not have functioned as well as it did.

Under the terms of Lend-Lease, when the war ended, equipment, including aircraft, had either to be returned or destroyed. Since the U.S. had enough problems just figuring out what to do with their own surplus airplanes, they didn't want the majority of Lend-Lease airplanes back, so most were destroyed. 2,000 Lend-Lease aircraft had to be dumped and the Fleet Air Arm was left with about 50 Fireflies and 100 Seafires. The rest - the American Corsairs, Avengers, Hellcats and Firecats - were thrown overboard out at sea or otherwise disposed of.

Friday 12th October 1945

Although there is no image, there is a page in Norman's photo book which is labelled and dated "Jenolan Caves, Blue Mountains, New South Wales." Presumably he had been given some leave and had taken the opportunity for more sight-seeing.

Wednesday 7th November 1945

Again, no image but another page in Norman's photo book is dated and labelled Perth, Western Australia.

The war ended so suddenly it was a huge challenge for the naval authorities to organise everyone and get them home. Admiral Sir Bruce Fraser, Commander of the British Pacific Fleet, and his top brass were concerned to keep up the morale of the personnel some of whom had been away from home for a long time and were desperate to get back. They went out of their way to keep everyone informed about dates for departure, visited ships and bases for pep talks and moved the ships about to keep interest levels raised. Maybe that's why Norman ended up visiting Perth before coming home.

Friday 9th November 1945 Returned to U.K.

The personnel of H.M.S. Nabaron (MONAB 4), including Norman's unit, embarked on H.M.S. Slinger which was anchored in Sydney harbour. They set off back home to the U.K. at 14.00 hours the next day and finally docked at Devonport (Plymouth, Devon) on Christmas Day 1945.

What awaited them at home? Rationing of petrol and food was even stricter than it had been in wartime. Job prospects were poor and with 2 million returning personnel unless your pre-war job had been left open for you, things were likely to be tough. Despite this, Admiral Fraser reported to their Lordships at the Admiralty that even regular naval personnel wanted to be made "hostilities only" or to buy themselves out.

And when they finally got home - was there a big parade? National church services to commemorate those who had given their lives serving in the British Pacific Fleet? A Pacific Campaign medal? No there was not. They came home and dispersed to their receiving stations and waited for their release date. The country did not want to know about the men who had served in the Pacific. They have been called The Forgotten Fleet and they were. No credit is given to those who organised The Fleet Train which was a great achievement with so many obstacles to overcome in such a short time. The main bases and technical and logistical support groups set up in Australia 12,000 miles from Britain despite huge shortages and after five years of war in Europe deserve equal credit. The contribution of those who served in the ships of the Fleet and the forward bases was acknowledged by

Admiral Rawlings, the second in command of the British Pacific Fleet, in his speech on 16th August 1945 when he paid tribute to those servicemen who had represented the Empire alongside the American Allies and who had given their all to ensure success. He questioned whether those at home had any idea of the strain caused by the long operational periods overseas and drew attention to the fact that so many of both officers and men were not much more than children, with Leading Seamen aged 19 years and Petty Officers of 21 years. Even Rawlings thought that if there had been the arrival in Britain of just a token returning force at the time of the Victory celebrations, the British Pacific Fleet might have been fixed more firmly in the public's memory. But it was not to be. In time the Fleet just faded away, with the result that it may have been the largest assembly of British ships in history but nobody either remembered or cared.

18th December 1945 - 3rd January 1946

Norman's service record shows that he was stationed at the transit camp H.M.S. Waxwing in Scotland.

4th January - 26th January 1946

During this period Norman's service record places him at H.M.S. Landrail located in Scotland on the western side of the Kintyre Peninsula. The base had an exceptionally long runway and was a former R.A.F. air station. It was opened as a naval base in 1941 but by early 1945 had become dis-used and kept operational on a care and maintenance basis only. It was re-activated during the Korean War for training purposes before becoming important during the 1960's for N.A.T.O. use during the Cold War. I can find no clues anywhere as to why Norman should have been stationed there for three weeks.

27th January - 31 July 1946

He then went to H.M.S. Blackcap, an airfield in the village of Appleton Thorn, close to the village of Stretton, south of Warrington in Cheshire. H.M.S. Blackcap was commissioned in June 1942 and forty one Fleet Air Arm squadrons were based there at various times. It had an operational capacity of 180 aircraft and a large hangar complex had been constructed for aircraft maintenance. At the end of the war many American Naval Aircraft were flown into Blackcap for disposal. As many of the Lend-Lease aircraft had been fitted with British radio equipment, it seems conceivable that it may have been Norman's job to remove the radio equipment before the aircraft were destroyed.

On 27th January 1946, while stationed at H.M.S. Blackcap, just a few months before he was de-mobilized, Norman was upgraded to Petty Officer losing the "Acting" designation (but it was still temporary).

At the end of July 1946 Norman was released from his service and given a civvy street jacket and trousers, a character statement from the captain and a war gratuity aka A Certificate of Post War Credit. Norman received a Class 'A' reference and £63.19s.6d (about £1,660 in today's money) for 1,355 days of service to his country. Out of this he had to pay his employer £9.15s 0d (£253 nowadays) for the contributions to the pension scheme he'd missed while he was away. He also took back to civvy street recurrent malaria which affected him on and off for the next ten years.

Norman was fortunate in that he was able to resume his old job at West Riding County Council. He was there for three months before going off to Bradford Technical College to study Public Health and Administration from which evolved a successful career as an Environmental Health Officer.

Acknowledgements

I read some really interesting books in the course of gathering knowledge and understanding for my annotations to Norman's World War II diary. These have included:

CHURCHILL W.S. The Second World War (six volumes) 1952 Cassell and Co.

CROSSLEY R.M. Commander 'Mike' D.S.C R.N. Up in Harm's Way: Flying with the Fleet Air Arm 1995 Airlife Publishing Ltd.

HOARE J. Tumult in the Clouds: A Story of the Fleet Air Arm 1976 Michael Joseph.

HOBBS D. The British Pacific Fleet: The Royal Navy's Most Powerful Strike Force 2011 Seaforth Publishing.

LONGSTAFF R. The Fleet Air Arm A Pictorial History 1981 Robert Hale.

PRYSOR G. Citizen Sailors: The Royal Navy in the Second World War 2011 Penguin Books.

WRAGG D. The Fleet Air Arm Handbook 1939 - 1945 2001 Sutton Publishing.

For background I have visited many websites related to World War II (notably WW2 Talk), the Royal Navy and the Fleet Air Arm, individual ships and innumerable histories. In addition I have looked at the websites of the Royal Navy Research Archives and The Fleet Air Arm Archives although there is precious little information about H.M.S. Spurwing and not a great deal of information about H.M.S. Nabaron (MONAB 4) either.

And finally,

Many thanks to my husband, Michael, for helping me to write this book; to my dad for keeping his diary safe until we were ready to read it; and to you, dear reader, for reading this book.

You might also like: "Cabbage and Semolina: Memories of a 1950s Childhood". For more details and to read a free sample visit the Amazon website.

If you like reading detective stories you might enjoy Michael's "A Single To Filey", his best-selling DCI Tony Forward novel. More details of this and his other books on the Amazon website

Cathy Murray

October 2016

Cabbage and Semolina: Memories of a 1950s Childhood

From Nylon Frocks and Cotton Socks to Carrier Bags and Nutty Slack, Cabbage and Semolina is a kaleidoscope of recollections and family stories drawn from a happy childhood in 1950s Britain.

A Single To Filey

Michael Murray

Detective Chief Inspector Tony Forward's hobby is directing amateur theatricals.

His latest production for the Sandleton-on-Sea Players is "The Cherry Orchard".

It's nearly midnight and he still hasn't completed the dress rehearsal. Then duty calls: a man with fatal head injuries has been discovered in a remote bay on the East Yorkshire coast.

The man's name is Mark Coulson and he's the Headteacher of a local primary school. But no-one seems able to explain why this respectable, professional man was at such an isolated spot so late at night. His wife is the most mystified of all.

Why were Mr Coulson's pockets empty? Sergeant Wilmott believes robbery was the motive. But if the killer had stolen Coulson's car keys why is his car still parked nearby?

Was Mr Coulson murdered by a jealous boyfriend or husband? That's what DC Diane Griffiths thinks. But Mr Coulson's Chair of Governors says he was a boring man whose only interest was his work.

With such a baffling case to solve how can DCI Forward find time for "The Cherry Orchard"?

All available from Amazon

Printed in Great Britain
by Amazon